ARE YOU LIVING YOU~~R~~
AND MEANINGFULLY ~~...~~

Do you ever feel that, no ~~matter what you achieve~~ or
achieve in your life, there's still something missing? Do you
and your partner sometimes feel more like roommates than
lovers? Does it ever seem like you're so busy working, raising
a family, and trying to get ahead that you don't have the time
or energy to enjoy your life as much as you know you should?

In *Real Moments,* bestselling author and renowned relationships expert Barbara De Angelis shows you how to experience
more fulfillment and true meaning in your life *now,* not when
you have more money or find the right partner or achieve
your perfect weight, but in this and every moment. She shares
profound insights and techniques for creating more real moments with your mate, your children, your work, and with
yourself, and offers tools for practicing everyday spirituality,
so that the process of living itself becomes sacred and filled
with everyday miracles. Discover:

+ How you may be sabotaging your own happiness, and how
  to stop
+ Why money, success, and even love won't bring you joy
  unless you learn how to have real moments
+ How you can transform your life overnight just by paying
  more attention
+ How to find and live your true purpose—no matter what
  your job
+ How to use your intimate relationship as a path for personal and spiritual growth
+ How to nourish your children's spirits and recognize your
  children as your teachers
+ How to experience everyday spirituality and tap into your
  own inner wisdom

REAL

MOMENTS

·

Barbara De Angelis, Ph.D.

A DELL TRADE PAPERBACK

A DELL TRADE PAPERBACK

Published by
Dell Publishing
a division of
Bantam Doubleday Dell Publishing Group, Inc.
1540 Broadway
New York, New York 10036

ISBN: 0-440-50729-4

Reprinted by arrangement with Delacorte Press

Printed in the United States of America

Published simultaneously in Canada

November 1995

10 9 8 7 6 5 4 3 2 1

This book is dedicated with love and gratitude
to my beloved husband,
Jeffrey James,
for blessing my days and nights with real moments
and helping me discover Heaven here on Earth,

and to my precious animal companion,
Bijou,
for being the embodiment of love and loyalty,
and for patiently teaching me how to walk slowly, play often,
and always be right here, right now. . . .

Acknowledgments

I would like to express my love and gratitude to the following people:

First, to my dear friend and literary agent, Harvey Klinger, for understanding why *Real Moments* needed to be written: Thank you for standing behind my vision, for supporting me in spreading my wings and flying to new heights.

To my publisher, Carole Baron: Thank you for your tremendous patience while I readied myself to write this book, and for your trust in my words and the message they contain. You continue to give me an opportunity to touch the hearts and souls of millions of people, and for that I am deeply grateful.

To Linda Riddle and Diana Soto, the directors of my companies: Thank you for letting me disappear for three months while I wrote this book, and for your phenomenal dedication to spreading our message of love and transformation.

To my personal assistant, Martha Cole, without whom I couldn't have finished this book in such a short time: Thank you for keeping the world out, keeping my life running, keeping me energized with your warm smiles and generous enthusiasm, and keeping me sane during some of the busiest months of my life. You have been my own personal angel.

To Mike Warren and Don Davidson of Inphomation, Incorporated: Thank you for believing in me and my work, and for giving me the tremendous opportunity to transform the lives of so many individuals and families through my television infomercial.

To Philip Saltonstall, for taking such a wonderful photograph of me for my book cover. Thank you for understanding why I wanted to shoot the cover in Sedona, Arizona, and for finding such a powerful and breathtaking spot to capture a real moment.

To Dottie Webster: Thank you for allowing Jeffrey and me to enjoy the solitude and sanctity of your home in Sedona so that I could write the last section of this book with a rested body and an inspired spirit.

To Elaine Reyna, my sister, my teacher, my friend: Thank you for your tender love and gentle guidance as I rediscover the ways of the Earth. Thank you for the gift of my name and for seeing who I really am. May our spirits always soar side by side.

And most of all, to my husband, Jeffrey: Thank you for respecting the silent inner journey I needed to take to write *Real Moments,* and for surrounding me with so much love that I felt safe to go deeper than I have ever gone before. Thank you for honoring my new direction and for always traveling by my side. Thank you for crying at all the right places when you read each chapter. Thank you for making me your bride. You are my greatest blessing.

Contents

ix

Part Three
✦
REAL MOMENTS AND RELATIONSHIPS

Part Four
✦
THE PATH TO REAL MOMENTS
TOOLS FOR CREATING MORE LOVE
AND MEANING IN YOUR LIFE

Introduction

I wrote this book because I needed its lessons and reminders for myself. I wrote it because my life, like so many lives, needs more real moments. I wrote it because, as an author, I know that my most powerful path of self-discovery has always been to become silent, to listen to the silence, to write what I hear, and to know that the words which come through me onto the page are meant first for me to learn from, and then, for others to enjoy if they wish.

There are times in our lives that are ripe for reflection and transformation, and this is one of those times for me. Over the past few years, I have achieved much of the success I've always wanted. I've found the relationship I always dreamed of. I've created a rich and wonderful life. And yet, when I would ask myself, "Barbara, are you happy?" I found I did not know the answer. Friends would call to congratulate me on my accomplishments or my marriage, and say "You must *really* be happy *now*," and for days afterward, I would be haunted by their comments. I knew I *should* be happy with so much goodness in my life, but I suspected that I was not.

It was then I began to understand that what was missing from my life were more "real moments," moments when I was not trying to get somewhere or be something, moments when

I was fully experiencing and enjoying where I was, now. I had become very good at *doing*, but wasn't very good at just *being*, and of course that included *being* happy.

As I shared my secret handicap with friends and acquaintances, I realized that I was far from alone in my experience. "I'm writing a new book called *Real Moments*," I'd tell them. And everyone would respond in the same way: "Boy, do I need to read that!" I started seeing that I was not the only one standing at an emotional and spiritual crossroads in my life, that many of us are at that same crossroads, looking back on the life we have been living, questioning its meaning, questioning the choices we have made, searching for answers that will give us peace.

I believe too that, as a nation, America *itself* is in the midst of spiritual crisis, desperately trying to discover and define new values as it becomes apparent, in these violent and often frightening times, that the old values have somehow led us away from the very harmony and contentment our forefathers came here seeking. As we approach the twenty-first century, we are all, collectively, and alone, searching for more real moments.

In this book, I invite you to ask yourself the same questions I have been asking myself as I've stood at my crossroads:

"Am I happy?"
"What have I *really* been doing here?"
"Am I doing what I came here to do?"
"Do I have enough real moments in my life?"

I'll be honest with you—these are not always easy questions to confront. It takes courage to ask them, and often, even more courage to be willing to hear the answers that will emerge from your own heart. But your efforts will be rewarded by the new levels of love, peace, and revelation you will experience daily.

In the process of answering these same questions, I have discovered new and liberating truths about myself, and made powerful changes in my life, some quiet and invisible, and some quite dramatic. But the greatest change of all is that I am having many real moments now. More and more each day, I am discovering the peace I was searching for, and beginning to understand and experience what true happiness really is.

So even though this writing has been first for me, I offer it, in love, to you. My hope is that by sharing it with you, my fellow traveler, I will have enriched your journey toward your own real moments.

Barbara De Angelis
February 1, 1994
Los Angeles, California

Part One

THE HUNGRY HEART

Searching
for Real Moments

◆

· 1 ·

YOUR QUEST FOR HAPPINESS

"First I was dying to finish high school and start college.
And then I was dying to finish college and start working.
And then I was dying to marry and have children.
And then I was dying for my children to grow old enough for
    school so I could return to work.
And then I was dying to retire.
And now, I am dying . . . and suddenly I realize I forgot to live."
                                            — ANONYMOUS

This is a book about the real moments that make life matter, and how to have more of them. It is about experiencing fulfillment and meaning in your life *now,* not when you have more money, or find the right partner, or achieve your perfect weight, but in this and every moment. It is about how to rediscover real moments with your mate and your children, real moments with your work and your play, and, most of all, real moments with yourself.

All of my previous books have been about the relationships men and women have with one another. *Real Moments* is about the relationship we have with the process of living itself, and the peace many of us have been searching for, whether we're aware of it or not.

✦

Look honestly at your own life. Are your days and nights spent doing things that are meaningful and make you smile? Or do you spend the majority of your time doing things that give you back the smallest percentage of joy? When your life is over, will you wish you had spent your time differently? If you had only one month to live, what would you change?

✦

Look deeply into your own heart. Are you happy? Is there something you think needs to happen *before* you can be happy? Are you sure that if that something occurred, you would truly be happy then? Would it be enough?

✦

Look closely at the values of your spirit. If you suddenly died tomorrow, and you looked back on your life, what moments would you cherish the most? What would you miss the most about your time on earth?

✦

In writing this book, I offer you an opportunity to begin finding the answers to these questions for yourself as I have been doing for myself. I believe that asking ourselves these questions is very important. It forces us to stop living our lives mechanically and unconsciously, and demands that we *pay attention.*

There's a famous Zen story about the student who approaches his Master and asks him to share some words of wisdom about life. The Master looks intently at the anxious disciple for a moment, and then writes one word with his brush: "Attention." The disciple is confused, and nervously asks the Master to elaborate and the Master writes again: "Attention." By this time, the young student is beside himself

with frustration—he can't figure out what his teacher is trying to tell him. And once more the Master patiently writes:
ATTENTION . . . ATTENTION . . . ATTENTION

Paying attention to the moments in your life as
they unfold is what having real moments means,
moments when you are fully present, fully
feeling, fully alive.

Sometimes they will be moments of great happiness. Sometimes they will be moments of profound sorrow. But always, when you pay attention to where you are and what is going on, right now, you will experience a moment that has meaning, a moment that matters, and that is what I call a real moment.

✦

"I find the question 'WHY ARE WE HERE?' typically human. I'd suggest 'ARE WE HERE?' would be the more logical choice . . ."
— LEONARD NIMOY
Mr. Spock in *Star Trek*

Are you fully here, right now, reading this sentence? Or are you reading and thinking about the work you should be doing, or what you're going to have for dinner? Are you kind of reading, but also worrying about the argument you had with your lover last night, or whether the guy you just met will call and ask you out? Most of us are not very good at giving all of our attention to whatever activity we're involved in, at surrendering fully to the experience of the moment. Having real moments is difficult when we spend so much time NOT being in the present, for part of what makes a real moment so powerful, so fulfilling, is that you are experiencing it one hundred percent.

Another term for this is *"mindfulness."* Mindfulness is a

concept that is an integral part of many Eastern spiritual traditions, particularly Buddhism. Simply put, it means to *pay complete attention to whatever you're doing, to allow your "mind to be full" of the experience.*

Mindfulness delivers you fully into the moment. It can turn an ordinary experience like taking a walk, putting your child to bed, holding your partner close, or even driving your car into a real moment. When you are being mindful, your intention is to fully experience where you are and what you are doing, rather than to have what you're doing now be another passing, forgettable moment which comes after what you just did, and before what you're about to do. Later in this book I'll share some tools for living more mindfully

The opposite of mindfulness is *mindlessness*, to do things without thinking, without feeling, automatically and unconsciously. I believe that it is our mindlessness that causes much of our suffering and the suffering of those around us:

✦ Mindlessness is what allows you to stay in a relationship that isn't nourishing you, and may even be harming you, and not notice how miserable you are.

✦ Mindlessness is what allows you to ignore messages your body is trying to give you when it has chronic indigestion or heartburn, and, instead, to pop an antacid into your mouth, until one day years later the doctor diagnoses you with a serious disease.

✦ Mindlessness is what allows you to smoke, or drink, or do drugs, and not notice, in spite of your chronic cough, your emotional inconsistency, or your mental ups and downs, that you are slowly killing yourself and hurting the people you love.

✦ Mindlessness is what allows you to know that there is injustice and cruelty occurring in the world around you, but not to speak out against it or do anything to stop it.

Mindlessness is an unhealthy mental habit many of us suffer from too much of the time. When we live our lives mindlessly, we miss all of the real moments. Psychology professor Ellen Langer, who writes about mindfulness, says people who live and act mindlessly run the risk of "being trapped in unlived lives." We move through our days, months, and years, focusing not on where we are, but on where we are going, and then wonder why we never feel we arrive anywhere that brings us lasting fulfillment.

How We Postpone Happiness

It is easy to be mindless in America, because dreaming of and living for a better tomorrow is the American way. America has always been a place where people come to chase their dreams. Dreamers from all parts of the world emigrated here, and were encouraged to dream even bigger dreams. The problem is, in the second half of the twentieth century, we have gotten so good at living for tomorrow that most of us spend very little time in the present. We plan for or worry about the future, and before we know it, our life is over and we realize that we were too busy being preoccupied with what had already happened or what we wanted to happen that we forgot to enjoy what was actually happening in each and every moment. *We become experts at preparing to live, but have a difficult time fully enjoying the process of being alive, right now.* We prepare for our careers, we prepare for the holiday season, we prepare for the weekend, we prepare for our retirement— when you add them all up, we are preparing for our life to be over.

The problem with being so good at living for the future is that we *get in the habit of not being in the moment,* so when those wonderful events we've planned for actually occur—the vacation, the promotion, the party, etc.—we have no idea how to enjoy them. We rush through these long-awaited experiences as if we can't wait to get them over, treating them like another task to be dealt with, and then wonder why we are left feeling so let down, so unfulfilled.

Recently, a good friend of mine got married. She spent almost a year planning her wedding, which was a very elaborate and beautiful affair. The morning after the ceremony, she called me from the airport on her way to her honeymoon. When I asked if she was happy with how things had turned out, she confessed that she was feeling strangely empty. "I hardly remember the wedding," she commented in a disappointed voice. "It seemed to pass by in a blur."

My friend's experience is not uncommon:

> When we spend our lives preparing for the future, rather than enjoying the present, we end up postponing happiness. We lose our ability to appreciate and experience joy, so when we do have the opportunity for real moments, we miss them.

In America, we live in a culture that values *doing*, and not *being*. So it is no wonder that we are not good at creating and delighting in real moments. We have been concerned with quantity rather than quality, with the stimulation of constant activity rather than substance. We often judge ourselves and others on what we have accomplished, rather than on who we are. We are movers and shakers, achievement junkies, "a society of speed-worshippers," as Nina Tassi calls us in her book *Urgency Addiction*. "Bigger Is Better . . ." "All You Can Eat . . ." "Two for One . . ." "More for Your Money . . ." "Faster than Ever . . ." "New and Improved . . ."—these are concepts that make up the American psyche.

Since World War II, we have been in an era of frenzied

consumerism. We wanted to get as much stuff as possible as fast as we could. Consumption and accomplishment have been held up as the keys to happiness. We told ourselves that if we had the car, the house, the color TV, the right job, we'd made it. And if we had a newer model of these than the guy next door, or a more prestigious position, we were a success. Our heroes became those people who had the most. Our values focused on things. *Our goal was having and accomplishing instead of living.*

This "consumption consciousness" inevitably turned us into experts at postponing happiness. Postponing happiness means believing that, in order to be happy, certain conditions must be met. You think to yourself: "I'll be happy when . . ."

I'll be happy when I find the right partner.
I'll be happy when I lose twenty pounds.
I'll be happy when my kids are married and successful.
I'll be happy when I have my own business.
I'll be happy when I redecorate my living room.
I'll be happy when my boss finally gives me a promotion.
I'll be happy when I buy a new car.
I'll be happy when . . . you fill in your own blanks.

We believe that when we have a certain experience, or get a certain possession, or achieve a certain status. we will finally be happy and not until then. So we work hard, or allow time to pass, and eventually, what we thought would make us happy occurs. We finish school, or lose the weight, or open our own business, or buy the house. Then we wait to be overcome with joy—and we are disappointed. **We may feel a sense of satisfaction, but we don't feel happy.**

And so the process starts all over again. "Well, I know I said if I became company manager I'd be happy, but now I realize what will *really* make me happy would be to become a supervisor." And so once again, we postpone our happiness until we can achieve the next goal.

Like all addictions, the need to have enough and do enough requires increasingly larger doses to get you high, until you're just not getting off anymore. And for many of us, that is precisely what has been happening. We've bought our cars and our condos; we've launched our careers and climbed up the success ladder. We've tried to give our children the luxuries we didn't have growing up. We've gotten many of the things we wanted, and become many of the things we hoped for. But slowly, we have begun to suspect that something is wrong, *that the kind of dreams we've been following have delivered us into a spiritual and emotional dead end:* **We have been substituting the possessions we collected and the goals we achieved for real moments, and in spite of it all,** *many of us are not happy.*

What makes this process even more frightening is that the time in our life seems to fly by. Each Friday evening arrives and we wonder where the week went. Each New Year's Eve comes, and we wonder where the year went. We wake up one day and realize that we are turning thirty, or forty, or beyond, and wonder where all the time went. We watch our children graduate from school, or start families of their own, and feel like it was just yesterday that we rocked them to sleep or taught them to tie their shoes.

We cannot technically slow time down. We are changing, and ultimately aging and dying from the moment we are born. But by experiencing more moments completely and consciously, I believe we will also experience time in a more meaningful way.

The Longest Forty Seconds of My Life

You've probably had moments in your life that seemed to take hours, weeks that seemed to go on for months, months that seemed to last a lifetime. These are almost always times when you are fully feeling and experiencing what is happening to you—you are in labor giving birth to a child; you are waiting for test results to see if you or a family member is ill; you are sharing your first intimate kisses and embraces with a new lover; you're spending a night watching the phone, hoping your partner calls you to make up after a fight. In these situations, time appears to have slowed down, and no matter how much your intellect knows that this day, this night, is no longer or shorter than any other, you could swear that everything is moving at half speed. That's because you are intensely present, and intensely feeling, in each moment.

On January 17, 1994, at 4:31 A.M., I, along with millions of other Southern Californians, experienced one of the largest earthquakes in American history. I will never forget the terrifying sensation of holding on to our bed as it and the whole house violently shook and rumbled in the cold darkness. It felt and sounded like the end of the world had arrived, and we were certain that we were going to die. Thank goodness, we did not. And as we huddled together on the floor of our closet for the next few hours, riding out the aftershocks, we couldn't believe what we were hearing on the radio: All reports said the quake had lasted approximately forty seconds. "That's impossible," my husband and I said to each other. "It was *at least* three minutes." We thought the news reports weren't accurate. But they were. And in the days that followed, not one of the dozens of friends and neighbors I spoke with, nor the radio and TV commentators I listened to, had experienced a forty-second earthquake. They, like us, were certain that the initial temblor had continued for several minutes. Of course, we were all wrong. What we had experienced was the longest forty seconds of our lives.

The earthquake was, without doubt, the most frightening experience I've ever had. It certainly qualified as a real moment, though not the kind I choose to have often! However, like all real moments, it presented us with many gifts— couples became more intimate, having been reminded of what is really important in life; families drew closer together; friends and strangers reached out toward one another with true compassion and community. Experiencing that moment so intensely opened our hearts and woke up our spirits. **Because we were forced to slow down, we became completely present in each minute of that day and the days that followed, and as a result, we were able to feel more love.**

My Search for Happiness

For as long as I remember, I have been a seeker. Those who knew me would never have described me as a carefree, lighthearted little girl. My parents had a very unhappy marriage, and even as a child, I was looking for answers to explain the sadness I saw in my mother's eyes, the confusion I saw in my father's heart, and the pain I felt in my own. To the surprise of my teachers, my first poems written in third grade asked why there was so much unhappiness in the world. I had a burning need to understand the meaning of life, and felt lost without the answers I knew were missing.

As soon as I left home at eighteen, I began my search for truth in earnest. I found a spiritual teacher and began practicing meditation, spending months at a time in retreat, looking within for the peace and wisdom I longed for. After many years of focusing only on my inner world, I knew it was time for me to fully return to the outer world, and to discover my purpose for being here. That's when I went back to school to obtain my degrees, and began studying what I cared the most about—love, relationships, and the process of living.

I gave my first workshop in my living room for eighteen of my closest friends. I wasn't planning to become well known, or have a TV or radio program, or even write a book. I was just sharing what I'd been learning with people I loved. So I was surprised when thirty-five people showed up for the next workshop, and more for the next. Soon, it became clear that my path was being laid out before me, and that I should follow it, so I did. I felt very fortunate that I'd been blessed with the ability to communicate with people and remind them, along with myself, about the importance of love.

Once I made the decision to become a teacher, I committed myself to doing whatever I could to positively affect as many people as possible. I was not an overnight success, but I didn't expect to be. Nothing has ever come to me easily in life. I've always had to work very hard for whatever I got, and my career has been no exception.

Looking back, I think there are two reasons I have always tried so hard at everything I've done. The first is that when I was young, I had a lot less than most of my friends. Our house was the smallest of everyone in my crowd; my clothes were from the discount stores and had the labels cut out. I was never deprived of anything I really needed, but I did not know what it was like to have many of the things I wanted. So if I got something, it was because I had worked for it. The second reason I decided that I needed to try harder is probably because I felt so unattractive. Imagine a skinny, serious little girl with braids, sallow skin, and ugly white glasses, and you'll get the picture. I knew I wasn't about to impress anyone with my looks, so I figured I'd be smart instead. Even years later, when I got contact lenses, learned to style my hair, and knew there were boys who found me appealing, I had a hard time feeling like I looked O.K.

So as my career began to take off, I was too busy trying hard and working nonstop to notice that I was achieving a lot of success. Then, a few years ago, I had an experience that began to change the course of my life. It happened while I was being driven to the daily television show I was doing at the time. A friend from out of town was with me, and as we pulled up to the studio and she noticed some fans waiting for my autograph, her face broke into a wide smile. "You really made your dreams come true, Barbara," she said with love and admiration. "You must really be happy."

When I heard her words, it was as if a curtain had suddenly been lifted from my mind. In that moment, I saw that I had, indeed, achieved most of the dreams I'd always believed in: I lived in a home nicer than any of the ones my friends had lived in when I was little; I could buy myself all the things I couldn't have as a child; I could send my mother on all the trips she could never afford while she took care of me; I'd finally found a man who loved me as much as I'd always wanted to be loved (even when he saw me in my glasses and a ponytail!). And here I was, driving up to my own television show. But when I looked deep into my heart, I realized the frightening truth—*I was not happy.* I was *satisfied* . . . I was *fulfilled* . . . but I was *not happy.*

For the rest of that day, and many days afterward, it was all I could think about. "How had this happened?" I wondered. I believed so deeply in the work I did, and I knew that it was making a difference in people's lives. I *was* proud of all I had accomplished in my career. I had a wonderful, loving relationship. I was healthy. Why wasn't all this making me happy? Why wasn't it enough? What was missing?

Slowly, as the days and weeks passed, I began to see the truth. *I was not happy because I had not been allowing myself to experience enough real moments,* moments when I wasn't trying to achieve anything, moments when I wasn't working toward a goal, moments when I was simply being right where I was. **I was an expert at doing, but I was not very good at just being.** For so many years I had believed that I would be happy when I got what I wanted. Now that I had what I'd thought I wanted, I knew that getting more of it would never make me happy. *If it wasn't enough now, it would never be enough.*

I didn't want to forget this insight, so I wrote out a sign and put it up on my mirror where I could see it each morning. The sign said:

W̲hen will I know I have enough,
and what will I do then?

These are powerful questions to ask yourself. If you don't feel you have enough right now, when will you have enough? How much money or success would it take until you felt you had enough? And then, what would you do? What would your life be about? I've had people tell me that just asking themselves these questions started a self-discovery process that went on for weeks.

The Difference Between Happiness and Satisfaction

I know now, because I've answered these same questions, that I could write a dozen more successful books, appear in hundreds of TV shows, or, if I had children and were a full-time mother, I could raise the perfect kids, or if I were in business, I could buy every company I wanted, but that none of these would make me happy. *They would hopefully satisfy and fulfill me, but they would not bring me happiness.*

What's the difference between happiness and satisfaction? Satisfaction is a kind of **mental contentment.** *It marks a completion of something you started with a purpose in mind*—a project, an interchange, a meal. For instance, I feel satisfied when I finish writing a chapter of my book. I feel satisfied when I give a speech and it is well received. I feel satisfied when I clean out my closet. Something is complete.

Happiness is more of an emotional contentment. I feel happy when I praise myself for what I wrote in that book chapter. I feel happy when I allow myself to feel the heart of someone who comes up to share with me after the speech. I feel happy when I look at a garment in my closet and allow myself to recall how much fun I had the night I wore it.

I remember the day when my third book hit #1 on *The New York Times* best-seller list. My agent called me early in the morning with the news, and of course I was very excited. I'd worked very hard on the book, and felt very fulfilled and satisfied that it was doing so well. Later that night after Jeffrey got home from work, we lay in bed together. As he held me in his arms, he stroked my hair and told me how proud he was of me for putting so much of myself into that book, for doing such a good job of promoting it on tour, and for being so smart. My eyes filled with tears as I received his love. In that moment, and not before, I was happy. That moment of love was a real moment.

We all accomplish things in our lives that bring us satisfaction. But no matter how much we do, or how much satisfaction we experience, we need to learn how to create real moments in order to be truly happy.

Happiness can only come from having
enough real moments in your life.

✦

Right around the time I was going through these changes, I traveled out of town to give a lecture. I shared my new realizations, as fresh and unformed as they still were, with my audience, because I learned a long time ago that it's easier to give a good presentation when you're being totally honest. After my talk, a woman approached me and gave me a big hug. "What was that for?" I asked.

"It was a thank-you, " she replied. "Tonight you freed me from some guilt that has been plaguing my heart for months."

She went on to tell me that she was thirty-nine years old, married, and the mother of three children. She and her husband lived a very comfortable life, and although she was far from wealthy, she felt very blessed. "But something happened to me right after I turned thirty-nine, " she explained. "I woke up one morning and realized that I wasn't happy. I've been so confused, because I love my husband and I love my children, and I have everything I ever thought I wanted. I always believed that would be enough to make me happy. I began wondering if my feelings of emptiness and restlessness meant that I wasn't really as in love as I told myself I was. I've been afraid to even talk to my husband about it, but he's been worried sick, because he can tell something is wrong. Until I heard you tonight, I didn't know what it was. But now I do."

Like me, like so many of us, my new friend had created a full and good life for herself, but she'd been too busy *doing* to stop and experience the small moments of happiness that surrounded her. She had forgotten how to connect with her husband. She'd forgotten how to take time to savor all of the gifts she'd been given. The reason she felt so empty was because she wasn't filling herself up with the love and meaning that were already there in her life. Her heart was hungry for more real moments.

✦

Here is what I have discovered about happiness:

Happiness is not an acquisition—it is a skill.

We do not experience happiness because of what we get. We experience happiness because of how we live each moment. It is a skill, an ability we must master, just like learning how to be a good painter, or an excellent athlete. Having an easel, a brush, and a palette of colors does not make me a painter—knowing how to paint does. Having a tennis racquet and ball does not make me a tennis player. Knowing how to play does. *Having certain experiences does not make me happy—knowing how to live them with full awareness and to mindfully be in each moment will make ..ie happy.*

In this way, happiness is only possible and available in the present moment, and from moment to moment. It comes to us *not* when we are searching for it, for then we are somewhere else other than here and now, but rather when we allow ourselves to be mindful of exactly where we are and fully experience whatever we are doing.

The word *"happiness"* comes from the old English word *"hap,"* which means chance or fortune (either good or bad) that befalls a person—in other words, what *"happens"* to someone. Happiness, then, literally means *the experience of being with whatever is happening.* So although when we say "I want to be happy," we are usually projecting ourselves into the future, happiness, by definition, can only be found now, in this moment.

Thich Nhat Hanh, a world-renowned Vietnamese Zen Master, has written an enlightening book called *Peace Is Every Step.* In it, he says:

> *"Life can be found only in the present moment. The past is gone, the future is not yet here, and if we do not go back to ourselves in the present moment, we cannot be in touch with life."*

If you can't be happy now, with what you have and who you are, you will not be happy when you get what you think you want. If you don't know how to fully enjoy $500, you won't enjoy $5,000, or $500,000. If you can't fully enjoy taking a walk around the block with your mate, then you won't enjoy going to Hawaii, or to Paris. I'm not saying that having

more money or more recreation won't make your life easier—it will. *But it will not make you happy, because it can't.*
Only you can do that by learning to live with more real moments.

Imagine that you want to be a concert violinist. Someone
gives you an old, poorly made violin on which to practice. Of
course, you wish you had a Stradivarius, the best violin in the
world, but you don't. So you study day and night, you pour
your heart and soul into playing that inferior violin well. One
day, a benefactor appears and hands you the Stradivarius you
always dreamed of. Your hands shake as you pick it up, and
then you begin to play, and you play exquisitely. The reason
you can play so beautifully is not because you're using an
instrument that is worth $250,000. You play so well because
you had developed your *skill* as a violinist.

If you had not learned how to play that old, secondhand
violin properly, you would not have been able to play the
Stradivarius.

> If you don't develop your skill at enjoying what
> you have, you won't be any happier
> when you get more.

"And a Child Shall Lead the Way . . ."

Before you start thinking that this all sounds too esoteric
and abstract for you to grasp, let alone put into practice, I
want to remind you that you used to be an expert at happiness—when you were a small child. Children are masters at
creating real moments. They haven't yet learned to postpone
joy, so they practice it as much as possible! This is what
makes each child so magical. They are totally present, totally
alive in the moment. Their days and nights are filled with
constant laughter and celebration. It's not just because they

don't have jobs and bills and responsibilities—their priorities may be different, but they often play as hard and intensely as we work. Their contentment comes from their ability to discover and enjoy the pure wonder available in each taste, each flower, each cloud, each experience.

There are some people in your life you never forget, even if you encounter them just once. Several years ago I went to Disneyland with a group of friends. It was toward the end of the day, and we gathered on Main Street to witness the daily parade. As we waited for the characters and animals to appear, I noticed a woman push a little girl in a wheelchair up to the edge of the sidewalk so she'd have a better view of the festivities. She was about seven or eight years old, paralyzed from the neck down, and her wheelchair was more like a portable hospital with all kinds of boxes and devices attached to it that helped her body function.

Just then, the Main Street Parade began. Mickey and Minnie Mouse, Snow White and the Seven Dwarfs, and all the other colorful Disney characters danced down the street to the music of a marching band, followed by the star attraction—a huge gray elephant. But I hardly noticed the parade, because I could not tear my gaze away from the little girl. Her eyes were as wide as saucers; her mouth hung open in amazement; and on her face was the most radiant smile of joy I'd ever seen. She was spellbound by the spectacle passing in front of her.

My eyes filled with tears as I watched this special child, tears not of pity for her handicap, but tears of sadness for myself. I realized standing on that make-believe street that I did not know how to enjoy the magic of life as I saw her doing. I did not know how to be as happy as she was allowing herself to be. I did not know how to enjoy the parade with as much delight as she felt. I might be able to walk and run and do many things she could never do, but she had something far more valuable: **She possessed the gift of joy.**

I've never forgotten that little girl, or what she taught me, because that experience was a Real Moment for me. I had connected deeply with someone else's spirit, even though we never spoke, and it had infused the moment with meaning.

Barry Neil Kaufman, cofounder of the Option Institute, has a wonderful saying: *"We weren't born unhappy. We learned to be unhappy."* That means we still have the talent for living in the moment within us, that we can unlearn our habits of mindlessness and begin to mindfully appreciate each experience of being alive. I believe that children are sent to us to be our teachers. When we witness them feeling and experiencing so fully, we should remember that they are demonstrating powerful spiritual techniques for our benefit! We need to honor them as they lovingly remind us of the path we must travel to reclaim our own joy and find our own real moments. *"Except ye be as little children, you cannot enter the kingdom of Heaven."*

How I Learned to Stop "Climbing the Lake"

I did not find it easy to begin inviting real moments into my life. My old patterns of trying to do things kept getting in the way, and sometimes still do. A few years ago, around the time I first became aware of my difficulty in experiencing real moments, my husband, Jeffrey and I took a trip to New York City to do some business and have some fun. We arrived on the red-eye Friday morning, and as soon as we checked into the hotel, I found myself calling restaurants to make our reservations for the weekend, and scanning the paper for different activities we could enjoy. Jeffrey seemed to be a little annoyed with me, but I figured he was just tired. We went out for a while, and then came back to get ready for dinner. When

I took out my list of plans and began going over it with him, I was surprised that he responded by acting disinterested and aloof.

"What's wrong, honey?" I asked.

"I'm just feeling a little upset with you, that's all."

"Why, what did I do?" I asked defensively.

"I don't know, you're so frenetic, making lists and plans. Why can't you just relax and stop controlling everything?"

My red flag went up—he'd said the "c" word—"control."

"I'm not trying to control things, I'm just trying to make sure we have a good time!" I snapped.

"Well, stop trying so hard, Barbara, and maybe you will have a good time."

Suddenly, I began to sob, from a place deep inside of me. He was right: I was trying . . . trying to have a good time . . . trying to make everything perfect . . . trying to make him happy. I'd spent my whole life trying to control the outcome of the events around me, working hard to accomplish my goals, sincerely believing that the harder I tried, the happier I would be. Now I had come face-to-face with the truth—that *my trying itself was preventing me from experiencing the joy I had been so desperately searching for.* **And so I wept, for in that moment, I realized that I didn't know how to *not* try.**

Jeffrey came over and put his arms around me, and through my tears I whispered: "I'm afraid if I don't try, I'll miss something."

I will never forget what he said next:

"If you keep trying, you'll miss everything. . . ."

The power of the truth Jeffrey spoke penetrated deep into my heart. As he held me and kissed my tears away, I understood that I had to start learning how to live all over again. One kind of energy had taken me to this point of fulfillment in my life—the energy of doing: to push, to strive, to create. This was not a bad energy—it was necessary to help me achieve all I have. But I needed a totally new kind of energy to take me to my next level of fulfillment, a skill I wasn't very good at and hadn't known much about—the energy of being.

What my wise and sensitive man had seen that night in New York was that the very means I had used to get so far in my life were now getting in my way—that the more I tried to *do something* to be happy, the unhappier I, and certainly he, was going to be!!

Here is a story I wrote that night inspired by what Jeffrey taught me:

The Woman Who Tried to Climb the Lake

Once there was a woman who spent her whole life climbing a very high mountain. She began as a tiny child, and could not remember a time before the mountain. Year after year she would ascend the steep cliffs, and in the process she became very good at the motion of climbing. The muscles in her legs and her back grew strong, and after a while, climbing felt as natural to her as breathing. As time passed, and she went higher and higher, she didn't even have to try and climb any-more—her body did it automatically.

At last, one day, the woman reached the top of the moun-tain. She was overjoyed with her achievement, and couldn't wait to start out on the next portion of her travels, and to conquer her next mountain. As she looked out over the hori-zon, she saw a beautiful blue lake, stretching sideways as far as her eye could see. But being a climber all of her life, the woman had only lived on the mountains, so she had never seen a lake, and in fact, did not even know what a lake was. She watched the strange expanse before her, and concluded that it must be some unusual kind of blue mountain. Since the only way to continue her journey was to cross over the odd-looking blue form, she decided that was what she must do.

So the mountain woman walked up to the water, and began trying to "climb the lake" with the same motions she'd used to climb the mountain. At first, she couldn't understand why she wasn't making any progress, and, in fact, was exhausting herself. So she mustered all of the energy in her strong body and tried to "climb" even harder, placing one leg in front of the other, using her hands to attempt to grasp the "blue rocks." But her efforts were useless. She kept falling over, and wasn't going anywhere.

Just about this time, when the mountain woman felt like giving up, she noticed a person floating by on top of the blue lake, gentling gliding his body through the water with the slightest movements of his arms and legs.

"What are you doing, my friend?" he called out to her.

"What does it look like?" she answered, her face flustered with embarrassment. "I'm climbing the lake."

"Good woman," the man of the lake replied, "don't you know that you can't cross a lake by climbing it? The only way to travel through water is to swim."

"But I'm such a marvelous climber!" the mountain woman insisted. "I've spent my whole life learning to climb. I can climb any mountain, I can reach the top of any peak. Surely there must be some way I can climb the lake."

"I'm sure you are an excellent climber," the man of the lake answered politely. "But that skill won't help you here in the water. It took one kind of wisdom to get you to the top of the mountain—you had to make your power stronger than the mountain. Now you need to learn another kind of wisdom to get across the lake—you need to surrender to the power of the water and allow its force to be stronger than you. You don't have to try hard anymore. In fact, the less you try, the better you'll do!"

And so it was that the man of the lake taught the woman of the mountain how to swim. At first, she splashed and thrashed around in the water, for she was accustomed to using very strong energy in her climbing. But her teacher was very patient, and slowly she learned to float on the water's surface, and allow the waves and the wind to carry her gently forward, until she was hardly doing anything at all.

And that's how the mountain woman learned that the strength of surrender was just as powerful as the strength of pushing forward.

✦

As we learn to experience more real moments, we will be required to master different skills than those we've been using to live lives of list-making and goal-setting. **Climbing the lake doesn't work.** Throughout the rest of this book, I'll offer you tools for creating more real moments in every part of your life.

What Are Real Moments?

What is a real moment? How can you tell if you are having one? All real moments have at least three elements of experience that need to be present:

✦ Consciousness

Real moments occur only when you are consciously and completely experiencing where you are, what you are doing, and how you are feeling . . . *You are paying attention, so you will notice things you wouldn't normally perceive if you were not paying attention.* There is nothing else in your awareness but the experience you are having.

Only when your consciousness is totally
focused on the moment you are in can you
receive whatever gift, lesson, or delight that
moment has to offer.

✦ Connection

Real moments are always moments when you have made an emotional connection between yourself and something or someone else. It might be a connection between you and a loved one, or you and a stranger, or you and a tree you're leaning against, or you and God. *They are moments in which the usual boundaries which appear to separate us from one another are penetrated, and in that connection, a kind of magic occurs.*

We usually call this experience of melting
boundaries "LOVE." You and something else are
flowing into one another.

✦ Surrender

You allow real moments to happen when *you totally surrender into whatever you are experiencing, and let go of trying to be in control.* You are 100 percent engaged in what you are doing, whether it is taking a walk, making love, baking bread, or watching your children play. You are fully embracing, rather than resisting, the experience of the moment.

It is impossible to have a real moment
when you are trying to control or resist
a situation or emotion.

So, if I could give you a formula for having a real moment, it might sound something like this:

Become fully conscious of what you are perceiving or experiencing in this moment. . . .

Once you are conscious of it, allow yourself to break through the illusion of separation and make a connection with the person, thing, or feeling you've contacted. . . .

Then, surrender completely into that connection. . . .

Now, you should be having a real moment.

✦

Real moments are available in the things you already do every day. . . .

My brother is an expert windsurfer, and he has many of his real moments while he is standing on his board, riding the waves. All of his awareness is consciously focused on what he is doing. He feels totally connected with the sail in his hands, the fiberglass beneath his feet, and the water all around him. And he is surrendering completely to each movement of the wind and each spray of sea in his face. He feels fully alive, fully content. . . . He is one with the ocean.

My mother has many of her real moments in her garden. She focuses totally on each new flower she is planting, each patch of soil she is clearing of weeds, each old leaf she is plucking away. She makes a connection with the tiny, colorful lives that depend on her to be nourished and to blossom. And she surrenders to the feel of the earth between her fingers, the musky smell of the wet dirt that fills the air, and the sweet sensation of allowing Mother Earth to bring forth life through her.

I have many of my real moments while I walk my dog and best friend, Bijou. As I follow behind his small, furry body, I become totally conscious of every crack in the sidewalk, every bush and how its edges are shaped, every tree waiting to be visited. I connect with Bijou's relaxed pace of travel, and as I feel his rhythm, his needs become my own. And I surrender completely to the walk, knowing that there is nowhere else to go, and nothing else to do, for in that very real moment, Bijou helps me to remember that the purpose of life may be nothing more significant than to sniff each magical flower that we pass, and to enjoy the journey.

✦

Recently I received a greeting card in the mail, and I wanted to pass its message on to you:

Yesterday is history.
Tomorrow is a mystery.
Today is a gift.
That's why we call it "the present. . . ."

·2·

THE CRISIS OF SPIRIT
IN AMERICA

"There must be more to life than having everything."
— MAURICE SENDAK

How did we lose our ability to experience real moments? What is the source of the restlessness we sometimes feel in the secret part of our hearts? Why is it often so difficult for us to find the fulfillment we are searching for? To find the answers to these questions, and to properly begin our journey toward what lies ahead, we must first look back to the past.

So imagine for a moment that you are a time traveler from eighteenth-century America. You set the dials on your Time Machine ahead to the future, push the button, and when the machine stops, you look at the clock and discover that you've magically landed in the last few years of the twentieth century.

As you step out of your Time Machine, you are greeted by America as it is in the mid-1990s. The first change you notice is the tremendous advancement in technology—cars, airplanes, televisions, fax machines, dishwashers, computers— these are all miraculous to you. "How much easier life is now than it was where I came from!" you marvel to yourself.

But as you move among your twentieth-century relatives, you begin to notice many things that confuse you. First of all, the people you see do not seem to be as happy or friendly as you remember their being back home. They do not say hello to each other but instead walk swiftly by with anxious looks on their faces as if they are all rushing off to an emergency. "Has something terrible happened?" you ask a passerby. He shakes his head rudely, and turns away, leaving you to wonder why everyone seems so disconnected and agitated.

Soon you notice that the streets and parks are filled with refugees of some sort, hungry, frightened-looking adults, even children, who seem to have no place to sleep. You assume these must be the surrendered enemies from a recently fought war with a distant land, until you hear them speaking English. "Why are so many Americans living on the streets with no homes?" you wonder in disbelief. "And why is everyone ignoring them?"

But it is when you begin to read the newspapers and magazines, and watch the magical box they call television, that you become truly alarmed. For this is what you see and hear:

✦ "New statistics were released today, stating that last year 2.7 million cases of child abuse or neglect were reported."

✦ "A new survey found that 43% of the population either are alcoholics, grew up in an alcoholic family, or married an alcoholic."

✦ "Police now estimate that a woman is raped every six minutes in America, and that three out of four women will be victims of one violent crime during their lifetime."

✦ "The majority of homicides are committed by one loved one or relative against another, and not by strangers."

✦ "New studies reveal that approximately one out of every two marriages ends in divorce, and infidelity, especially among women, is on the rise."

✦ "The government reports that we are losing the war on crime, and projects a need for hundreds of new prisons to house the growing number of criminal offenders."

✦ "Another drive-by shooting was reported today in a small, quiet town in the Midwest. Three people were killed, and four were wounded. According to witnesses, the suspects did not know the victims, and their only motive for the killings was that they were in the mood to 'kick some butt.' "

You watch the news reports with horror. Random violence . . . Parents beating and molesting their own children . . . Children murdering other children . . . Millions of men and women destroying their lives with drugs and alcohol . . . Broken families . . . People living on the streets . . . And fear, fear everywhere. . . . *"What has happened to America?" you cry out in disbelief. "How did it turn into such a self-destructive society? What happened to the hopes we had in my time for a better future, the dreams we had for a nation of prosperity and peace?"*

And you rush back to your Time Machine and set the dial for the century you came from, praying that it's not too late for you to return, and weeping for your great-grandchildren's grandchildren who will one day be born into this civilization of lost souls.

✦

As we stand on the threshold of the twenty-first century, our nation exhibits every symptom of being in a profound state of emotional and spiritual crisis. What has happened to America? **We are a society dangerously out of balance:**

✦ We have more material comforts than any previous civilization, and yet we also show more evidence of personal unhappiness. Our levels of crime, abuse, divorce, and addiction, to name just a few problems, are higher now than at any time in the past, and growing worse each year.

✦ Our ability to technologically master our world continues to expand at a breathtaking pace, while our ability to successfully enjoy living in that world seems to have been lost. Experiences that we were brought up to believe we could take for granted have, for many of us, become distant dreams we recall with longing: marriages that last a lifetime; neighborhoods that are safe which we proudly call "home"; the confident certainty that our children will have a better life than we did; and perhaps most of all, lots of time—time to walk, to be quiet, to enjoy the fruits of our labors, time to do nothing or anything at all.

The result is a people searching desperately, sometimes even dangerously, but often unsuccessfully, for meaning. Those of us in our middle years are disappointed by and disillusioned with the deterioration of the safe world we knew when we were young. Our elders look nostalgically back at the past, remembering when things were perhaps simpler, but definitely more sane. And our children, to whom we will leave this turbulent legacy, are a generation already characterized by fear, anger, cynicism, and a loss of innocence.

We are *not* a society that is doing better and growing happier each day, and that was the American dream.

And then there is the crisis of the land itself: The earthquakes, the hurricanes, the fires and the floods, the icy winters that last forever, the rains that won't stop—the very body of our nation is out of balance. Scientists will, of course, have their logical explanations for these phenomena. But if you listen closely, you can hear Mother Earth crying out to us for help.

✦

Some part of you already knows all of this. Like our time-traveling friend, you have read the statistics in the papers; you have seen the reports on television; you or someone you love has already felt the shadow of violence or abuse or addiction or divorce or joblessness darken your life. You know that our world is not the safe and hopeful place it used to be. But like me, and like all of us, you turn away from your fear and your sadness, and, in turning away, develop a protective layer of numbness that allows you to go through your days without succumbing to despair. *And it is that very numbness that makes it difficult for us to experience the real moments that we need now more than ever.*

I believe that our emotional and spiritual survival is dependent on our NOT becoming numb, and on our NOT turning away. Of course, I have only told one side of the story. There is also much goodness in our nation, many powerful voices of caring, many forces of change. But they are not enough. Our country is in trouble. We, as a people, are in trouble. Your happiness, and the happiness of your children and their children is on the line. We cannot each single-handedly cure all of society's ills, but we can contribute more kindness, more caring, and more consciousness to what is happening inside of us and around us. And that will begin to make a difference.

The need for more real moments in our lives is more important now than ever before in our history—*moments of compassion toward our fellow human beings . . . moments of connection with those we love and those who need love . . . moments of centering and healing for ourselves.* Yet ironically, it is

more difficult to have real moments than it has ever been before. This is the dilemma we are faced with as the Millen-
nium approaches.

How did we get from our nation's hopeful beginnings to
this disheartening time? When we begin to understand the
historic roots of the crisis of spirit in our country, we will
understand the crisis of spirit in ourselves.

From Frustrated Pioneers to Novelty Junkies

America is a nation infused with a pioneer spirit. Many of
our ancestors left their homelands in all parts of the world
and traveled thousands of miles to this country, often braving
tremendous emotional, financial, and physical hardships. African Americans, who unlike the original settlers did not arrive here of their own free will, but were brought to our
shores in chains, have been forced to become pioneers of a
different sort. They have taken the painful journey from
bondage to freedom, moving out of the plantations and
through the states as they searched for the dignity and equal-
ity their persecutors stole from them. Even the indigenous
peoples of our land, the Native Americans, migrated across
the plains in search of favorable weather and good hunting.
*We have had a history of being movers, always fascinated with
what is over the next hill, always looking for more*—more land,
more water, more abundance, more freedom.

Around the beginning of this century, we realized that we
had moved to the limits of our borders. There was nowhere
else to physically go, no new cities to settle, no new space in
which to spread out. We were *frustrated pioneers* who had run
out of new frontiers. But we couldn't stop, because by this
time, **we'd become novelty junkies.** The addiction ran in the
family—it started with our grandparents or great-grand-
parents who first arrived here in the promised land, and had

been passed down to us. Now it was in our blood. *We were hooked on wanting more.*

And so we refocused our hunger for more from places to things, and our fascination with technology and consumerism began. We made things work faster and more efficiently. We built things bigger and better. We created new rules about how to live, what to buy, what to wear, what was "in," and when we quickly tired of these, we rebelled against the traditions we ourselves had recently established, and made even newer rules. *Our constantly changing tastes were what fueled the American economy.* Even if our old car ran just fine, we still hungered for the new model. Even if our old shoes fit, we had to have the new ones with the higher heel, or differently shaped toe. Even if our old TV worked well, we needed the new version with the improved remote control and additional features. Anything old we discarded, anything new we fell in love with.

It is inherent in human consciousness to improve. So there is nothing unique about a people searching for and creating ways to make their life better—all civilizations throughout history have done this. *What is unique about us in America is the accelerated rate at which we continually search for novelty and progress.* More elements change in our modern culture during one year than used to change in European or Asian cultures for decades. And once other countries learn about what is "hot" in the United States, they often throw aside age-old traditions and embrace our latest fad with open arms.

In this way, America and its worship of the new has radically transformed the face of the world. Blue jeans, T-shirts, tennis shoes, movie stars, rock and roll, hamburgers—these have been our cultural exports. You don't hear American teenagers singing Italian or German pop songs. You don't see Americans rushing by the millions to see the latest French blockbuster. You don't watch Brazilian television shows subtitled in English. Yet the reverse of these occurs every day on every continent.

On a recent trip to Bali, my husband and I were witnessing a cremation parade and ritual, which to the Balinese is a very sacred and joyous occasion. As we watched thirty young Balinese men lifting up the platform on which the deceased rested, we were amazed to see almost half of them wearing T-shirts emblazoned with the names and logos of American rock groups. The Balinese culture is dedicated to its ancient traditions which are an integral part of everyday life even today. And yet somehow, rock groups like Pearl Jam and Aerosmith had even invaded the cremation ceremony of a Balinese rice farmer.

The Self-Indulgent Years

The baby boomers took a temporary vacation from materialism during the 60s, rebelling against the status quo and trying to live a "tune in, turn on, drop out" philosophy. But once we found out how much fun it was to make and spend money, the guys eagerly threw on their suits and tied back their long hair, the gals shaved their legs and got back into their bras. And as we traded in our old Volkswagens for shiny new Hondas and Toyotas, we followed the example of our now overjoyed parents and entered the American mainstream with a passion.

Starting in the late 1960s and continuing into the 70s and 80s, our frenzied consumerism peaked. *"You can have it all"* was our mantra, and we believed it. We'd always been a society enamored with the concept of freedom—that is what drew many of us here. Now, political and religious freedom weren't enough. We wanted financial freedom, sexual freedom, and emotional freedom. We wanted as many things, as much pleasure, and as much self-discovery as possible.

As consumers, we could not purchase enough, invest enough, or borrow enough to satisfy our hunger. Fortunately for us, technological advancement was peaking as well, and entire new industries were born, from computers to fax machines to cellular phones to CD players. How did we plan to pay for all of our new stuff? Why, we just filled our wallets with credit cards and took out second mortgages on our homes. The government printed more money, and we went on spending it.

In our personal lives, our pioneer mentality expressed itself in our passion for breaking through the old boundaries and experiencing more individual freedoms than ever before. "Let it all hang out" and "Do your own thing" were the mottoes. Open marriage, one-night stands, and swinging were born as we turned away from the old traditions with the same fervor with which we once left the old country and came to America.

Some observers call this period of our recent history "the self-indulgent years." We wanted to have more, do more, and be more. The phrase "self-improvement" was born, and along with it came industries to help us be the best. Now we could join health clubs to have the perfect body, take seminars and listen to tapes to understand and motivate ourselves, and read books to make sure we were doing it all correctly. Our most popular bestsellers taught us how to have better sex, how to be better parents, better tennis players, better managers, better at everything.

The more we did, the more we realized that it takes a lot of time to excel. And so we bought organizers, studied time management, and scheduled ourselves carefully. Even our children, busy with their gymnastics lessons, hockey practice, and computer clubs, needed kids' daytimers to keep track of their activities.

Perhaps we were too busy playing with our new toys and achieving new goals to notice the symptoms of burnout as they began to surface. At first, they were subtle: We'd realize it had been weeks since the whole family had eaten a meal together; we'd look at the calendar and discover that we had no free days or weekends during which we could, heaven forbid, do nothing; and the credit card bills kept piling up. But hey, we were having so much fun, slowing down was unthinkable.

It is apparent that most of us aren't having fun anymore. Why? *We didn't pay attention, and now we are paying the price for our self-indulgence.* All parties eventually have to end, and ours was no exception. The glitz and greed of the 70s and 80s is over, and now we are coming to terms with the social, spiritual, and emotional costs.

The crisis we face today in the United States reflects several political, technological, economic, and social changes that hit us all at the same time and, together, have taken their toll on the American psyche.

The Demise of the American Dream

Economically, reality finally set in during the latter part of the eighties. We'd had a wonderful time spending money, but finally, the time for paying the bills arrived. You don't have to be a financial expert to know what happened, and it doesn't matter what word we use to describe it—Recession, Depression, National Debt. The bottom line is that we ran head-on into an economic crisis that is affecting all of us.

Part of the fallout has taken the form of unemployment, not a new phenomenon in the twentieth century. But this time, it's *who's* unemployed that has us so frightened. People who never expected to be laid off are jobless—top level executives, professionals, managers. *Time* magazine reported that fifty-eight percent of Americans either themselves have lost a job or have a friend who has lost a job since 1991.

It's not uncommon to see men and women in their late forties and fifties showing up at job interviews and temp agencies looking for work. It was one thing to be between jobs as a twenty-year-old with no responsibilities. It's quite another to have three teenagers at home, a mortgage, piles of other debts, and to find that the position you've held for ten or fifteen years has suddenly vanished. Most men went into their middle years with the goal of achieving financial independence, or of retiring early so they could enjoy the fruits of their labors. Now they just hope they'll still have a job to eventually retire from.

For many older Americans, even the once glorious dream of retirement has tarnished, as interest rates plummeted, and the investments senior citizens had counted on to support them for the remainder of their lives have become less and less valuable. Millions of people over sixty, who'd carefully planned for their "golden years," working ten-hour days so they'd be able to enjoy the good life, find themselves having to postpone retirement indefinitely in order to simply survive. Others live in constant fear of not being able to pay medical bills, or they are faced with the disappointing reality of never being able to take that trip they always talked about, or burdened by the sense of failure that they will not leave any financial legacy to their children and grandchildren, because they must use their savings to live.

The effect our ailing economy is having on the twenty-something generation is no less frightening. It used to be that young adults went to college in the first place knowing that they would be able to get a much better job with a degree than without one. Now they are lucky to get a job at all. We have a whole new subculture of bellboys, waiters, and taxi drivers with bachelor's and master's degrees. The hopefulness the younger generation felt in the seventies, when college graduates were aggressively recruited by major corporations throughout the country, has been replaced with a dark pessi-mism about the future. No longer do they believe, as so many generations before have, that they will be better off than their parents were. Instead, their hearts are clouded with uncer-tainty.

And then there are the baby boomers, now with children of our own, facing the disheartening knowledge that our sons and daughters will probably not grow up to have more than we did—that, in fact, they will be lucky to have as much as we do. We watch our children struggle to find work, we open up our homes to them when they move back in order to save money, and we hurt as we witness their worries about their futures, remembering when we were their age and believed that nothing could prevent us from having it all.

We try to tell ourselves things are not that much worse than they used to be, that tough times come and go. But then we drive down the street, or walk out of our office and see the homeless men, women, and children, hungry, hopeless, huddled in the cold—they are the human reminders that we live, indeed, in a time like no other. Yes, there are the alcohol-ics, the ex-convicts among those who sleep on the streets or in cars. But there are also the single mothers, the unemployed airplane mechanics, the kids whose dads lost their jobs of fif-teen years and didn't have any savings. Their faces reflect the human toll our economic crisis is taking. *It is not just about the loss of jobs, of homes, of opportunities—it's about the loss of the American dream.*

The Frantic Family Syndrome

Even for those of us who have jobs and can pay the bills, life is not what it was for our parents, or what we always thought it would be. Most families need to have two incomes in order to survive, and that means more women than ever before are working full- or part-time. Spending time with the children or with your partner, taking care of the home, pursuing hobbies or other interests, even doing the laundry—none of these are as easy as they used to be, because we are too busy surviving. This manic whirlwind of activity extends itself to our kids who, sensing that those who do more will get more, are scheduled weeks in advance for their own activities.

Psychologist John Rosemond has labeled this *"The Frantic Family Syndrome."* Mom, Dad, and the kids racing around from appointment to meeting, from school to work, occasionally stopping to eat, although rarely together. The home, which used to be a sanctuary of relative calm in the midst of our busy lives, has now, for many of us, become a domestic pit stop, the place we bathe, sleep, change our clothes, and grab some food before racing off to our next obligation.

Is it any wonder that we have lost our ability to have real moments when we are working so hard to hang on to what we still have? *We have been afraid to stop because we would end up with less . . .*

The Psychic Assault of Technology

If the American dream has been tarnished by our economic woes, then the American psyche has been equally injured by the explosion of technology. It is ironic that the very industry that brings us so much comfort and entertainment, and that has made our lives so much easier in a myriad of ways is itself responsible for much of the psychological dis-ease that has become a part of the American profile. From this point of view, the telecommunications satellite has been a weapon far more damaging than any of the warheads or missiles we once feared.

Modern technology has moved us out of the industrial age into the information age. Since we have become accustomed to our high-tech lifestyle, we rarely think about the impact it is having on us. I recently heard a sociologist on the radio share an amazing fact: *With the use of satellites, television, and computers, you and I receive more information in one day of our lives than our ancestors of several generations ago used to receive in 1,000 days!!* That means our brains have to process as much input in 24 hours as our brains used to process in 24,000 hours.

Fifty years ago, when World War II was fought, our parents and grandparents received their information about it through newspapers, radio, and film clips. Most of the news came without pictures, without sound, and often was days old. The death and destruction that accompanies all war lost some of its terrifying reality because there wasn't much **immediacy** to it. But today it is a much different story. **We don't just read about war, death, or natural disaster—we witness it as if we were there.**

In the past few years, I've had a front row seat at the crisis in the Persian Gulf, the war in Bosnia, the hurricanes in Florida, the floods in the Midwest, earthquakes in California and Mexico, and several shoot-outs between the United States government and various criminals. On just one day several months ago, I watched fires rage out of control in Los Angeles, a plane crash in Hong Kong, a bombing in Palestine, and children starving in Somalia. By pushing a button on my TV remote control, I've been able to be an eyewitness to tragedies that, in my own personal world, I would never encounter. This is too much pain for one person to absorb in a lifetime, let alone in one day.

What if our ancestors had been able to watch the dropping of the first atomic bomb in Hiroshima, or the executions during the French Revolution, or the spread of bubonic plague in the fourteenth century, or the crucifixion of Christ on TV?

Can we even fathom how this would have affected them and the decisions they made that determined our future?

America's Mental Meltdown

Observing even one of these horrific events would cause any human being great emotional distress. So how does it affect us when we are bombarded with them day after day? I believe it sends us into *major psychological overload*. The human psyche is only able to handle so much stress before it begins to malfunction, just as too much electricity flowing through a wire will cause it to melt, or even catch on fire.

Imagine a group of men in a room from which they cannot escape. Loud music blasts from dozens of speakers on the wall. Numerous television sets flicker with broadcasts from different channels. Lights constantly flash, and the room itself is vibrating. After just a short time, most of the men will begin to display severe changes in mood and behavior. They will become increasingly depressed, fatigued, and anxious. Soon after, they will start exhibiting signs of hostility and aggression. And eventually, the men will become violent. Nice guys will start screaming at one another, and even the most sensitive members of the group will get into physical fights.

What is happening here? *They are suffering from the effects of being overstimulated.* Scientific studies that investigate the effects of overstimulation on animals and humans reveal that when we are exposed to too much mental, emotional, or sensory input at once, our anxiety levels radically increase. **These high levels of anxiety need to express themselves somehow, and they often do in the form of hostility and violence.** It's as if our brains say: "STOP! I CAN'T TAKE IT ANYMORE. I FEEL LIKE I'M GOING TO EXPLODE!!"

All of us have experienced this in mild forms. Your phone rings, your tea kettle whistles, and your child asks you a question all at the same time, and you feel like screaming. Your mental circuits are overloaded, and your groan or curse indicates that you have just short-circuited.

We, in America, are suffering from *mental meltdown and emotional short-circuiting*. Our boundaries have been invaded by satellite television, fax machines, and cellular phones, and there are fewer and fewer places to hide. We can no longer ignore what is happening in other parts of the country or the world by retreating into our own private universe. **In our new global village, we are continually and relentlessly overstimulated, and this sentences us to living in a constant state of subtle but very real anxiety.**

Anxiety is not just a mental condition—it manifests itself in very powerful physiological changes. Our body gets hyped up when we experience fear or nervousness—blood pressure rises, heart rate increases, respiration becomes faster. It's as if our body releases its own brand of speed or uppers into our system. Perhaps we do not all become violent and show signs of overt hostility. But one side effect of constant stimulation is that *we get hooked on that hyped-up feeling, needing more and more of it to feel alive.*

Look at the trend in the popular television shows of the past few years: *Rescue 911, Emergency!, Cops*—we can't get enough of what we call reality-based programming. For anxiety junkies, it's not enough to be able to watch tragedies from around the world twenty-four hours a day on CNN. We want to see all the auto accidents, medical emergencies, heroic rescues, and dramatic arrests that we can. We need to keep that adrenaline pumping.

Of course, our other favorite type of program is the talk show, on which we watch everyday Americans vent their anger and hostility toward their mates who cheated on them, their parents who messed them up, and their neighbors whose dog is doing his business on their lawn. We see skinheads and African American separatists scream racial slurs at one another; we hear couples reveal the most intimate and embarrassing details of their unhappy sex lives. Ten years ago there were just two or three daytime talk shows on the air— now there are dozens. *It appears that we would rather become obsessed with other people's lives than fully live our own.*

Yesterday morning I turned on the television and watched a few minutes of a popular talk show. A couple sat on the stage yelling at each other. I could hardly understand what they were saying, since they were both screaming at the same time. The host of this program stood silently by, pretending to have lost control of the segment, but I know he must have felt some satisfaction as he pondered the high ratings this maniacal husband and wife would, no doubt, bring him.

I speak from experience, and with compassion for the hardworking hosts and producers of these programs, because I once hosted a talk show for a major television network. Day after day I would fight to produce a "quality" episode that would educate the viewer about relationships. I always received the same response—that "quality shows didn't get good numbers." I needed to book transvestite nuns, crossdressing dads, and women who only dated male strippers if I wanted to compete with the most popular programs.

The most recent contribution to our hunger for sensationalism is *Court TV*, an entire channel dedicated to live broadcasts of actual criminal and civil trials. Millions of Americans tune in each day to watch defendants sweat on the witness stand as they are grilled by the prosecution, and victims tearfully testify about their terrible experiences. We love speculating on people's guilt or innocence, and wait anxiously for each new development in these cases like a modern-day version of the lynch mob waiting for the horse to be kicked out from under the poor condemned man.

How America Has Numbed Out

What has technology done to our values, to our spirit?

By exposing us to so much human drama,
technology has desensitized us both to our own
pain and the pain of others.

As Vice-President Al Gore writes in his book *Earth in the Balance,* "Just as the members of a dysfunctional family emotionally anesthetize themselves against the pain they would otherwise feel, our dysfunctional civilization has developed a numbness that prevents us from feeling the pain of our alienation from the world." In other words, we've numbed out. Normal, everyday emotion isn't enough to make us feel passionate and alive anymore.

And so, we have become a nation of voyeurs. We get turned on by suffering and scandal. We get our kicks from watching physical and emotional violence, our entertainment from seeing strangers in psychological distress. We can moralize all we want about family values, but the bottom line is that, in late-twentieth-century America, *we are addicted to the shocking.*

Nowhere is this more apparent than in our nation's obsession with sex. Sex gets our attention like nothing else can, whether it's on the cover of a magazine, the plot of a television show, or the topic for a "tell-all" book. Journalist Neal Gabler believes that the increasingly graphic sexual explicitness found in our culture, from shock radio to MTV, is a *reflection of our frustration with the loss of the genuine."* "We feel a pervasive lack of authenticity in politics, art, religions, athletics, even human relations," he writes. "We no longer believe. Amid the fakery, we want something real. And just as the sex act itself rips through layers of inauthenticity to something fundamental, so, metaphorically speaking, does sexually explicit language . . . rip through . . . to something basic, primitive, and genuine."

What America Has Lost

I believe that we, as a nation, are not really numb at all. I think we're in a state of psychological shock, exhibiting all the symptoms of post-traumatic stress disorder. We have suffered many severe losses, all at the same time, and we are simply overwhelmed:

✦ *We've lost our confidence in the American dream.*

We can't count on the things we used to. We can't be sure that if we work hard all of our lives, we will achieve the financial security we want. We can't be sure that if we do well at a job, we won't be fired anyway due to the sluggish economy. We can't be sure that if we educate ourselves, we will even be able to find employment. *We can't be sure that if we play by the rules, we will be rewarded.* **Our sense of entitlement has been taken away from us, and that's what the American dream was all about.**

✦ *We've lost our belief in a better future.*

For the first time in centuries, the majority of us do not feel that the future will be better than the past. We don't believe that our children will be better off than we are. We don't believe that social conditions in our country will improve, rather than decline. Even the most idealistic of us has more dread and less hope than ever before.

✦ *We've lost our sense of safety.*

Even in small-town America, we no longer feel safe taking a walk at night, for fear that we will become yet another crime statistic. We don't feel safe driving our cars, for fear that we will be carjacked. We don't feel safe having sex if we are single, for fear that we will contract the AIDS virus. We don't feel safe sending our children to school, for fear that there will be a drive-by shooting, or an act of random violence. We don't feel safe leaving them in day care, for fear that they will be molested. We don't feel safe letting them ride their bikes to a friend's house, for fear that they will be kidnapped. We don't even feel safe in our own homes.

✦ *We've lost our escapes.*

When we lose our sense of safety, we also lose our traditional escapes from everyday stress and anxiety. Going out at night, taking a drive, having sex—all these were once ways we dealt with tension and focused on just enjoying life for an hour or two. Now even these activities can be dangerous, and we think twice before engaging in them. We feel trapped, prisoners in our own homes.

✦ *We've lost our psychic privacy.*

The old boundaries that separated our lives from those of the rest of the world have been invaded. Satellite technology has made it all but impossible to insulate ourselves from the world's tragedies and turmoil in our new, global village. It is difficult to "tune out" what is happening around us, even if we want to. And the phrase "I can't be reached" has all but disappeared from our vocabulary as cellular phones and fax machines make it possible for people to find us wherever we are.

✦ We've lost our protective distance from "the enemy."

Since our country was founded, Americans always knew who the enemy was. He was the British, the Japanese, the Germans, the Russians—that country and those people over there and far away. With the end of the Cold War, the downfall of communism, and widespread nuclear disarmament, our distant enemies have all but disappeared. Suddenly the threat to our home, our property, and our family is not coming from outside our borders, but from inside. The person with the gun out to get you is no longer around the world—he is around the corner. *The enemy has arrived—and he is one of us.* ...

✦

Each of these in itself is a powerful loss. Together, they are psychologically devastating. And like all losses, these evoke intense emotions in us—feelings of anger and powerlessness:

We are angry because we are overstimulated.

We are angry because things were always supposed to get better, not worse.

We are angry because we have been working so hard to do things right, and it seems like someone changed the rules without telling us.

And we feel powerless to protect ourselves and those we love from harm.

In times of crisis, it is always the weakest elements in society that begin to break down first. Perhaps, then, the epidemic of violence in our nation is an expression of this same powerlessness by those who didn't feel empowered to begin with. Perhaps the randomness of the violent acts honestly reflects the generalized rage of those who commit these crimes. All of us are victims of the times, but some of us, who started out at a disadvantage, are falling apart faster than the others.

"Who killed childhood? We all did."
— JERRY ADLER
Newsweek magazine

If we as adults are experiencing high levels of anxiety and despair in these challenging times, then God help our children, who, as *Newsweek* magazine wrote in a recent cover story, are "growing up fast and frightened." When I went to elementary school, my biggest worry was whether or not I'd get picked for a volleyball team in gym class, or if I'd get invited to Emily Bell's birthday party. Now kids worry about getting killed. Six-year-olds watch children their age die in drive-by shootings. Junior high and high school students pass through metal detectors to make sure no one is carrying a gun. Childhood is not what it used to be—it has lost its innocence, and in this way, it isn't even childhood anymore.

Don't think your children or grandchildren don't know what's going on. They do. They may even be more honest sharing their feelings about it than we adults are. A recent Princeton survey of 758 children aged ten to seventeen from all economic backgrounds came up with the following results:

- ✦ 56% feared violence against a family member
- ✦ 53% feared an adult losing his or her job
- ✦ 61% worry that they won't be able to find a good job
- ✦ Only one third said they would be financially more successful than their parents
- ✦ 47% feared not being able to afford shelter
- ✦ 49% worried about not having enough money
- ✦ Only 31% in the cities and 47% in the rural areas felt safe at night
- ✦ One in six has seen or knows someone who has been shot

Safety and trust have always been the hallmarks of childhood. They insulate children from the harsh realities that will come with adult life so that they can grow and learn with confidence. When our sons and daughters wake up to a world they cannot count on, and go to sleep in a world they fear, is it any wonder that one in seven of them has contemplated suicide? "Increasingly they [our children] are left to fend for themselves in a world of hostile strangers, dangerous sexual enticements, and mysterious economic forces that even adults find unsettling," explains journalist Jerry Adler. At least those of us who are older have had time to develop some coping skills that help us deal with our anxiety. But what are our kids supposed to do with theirs?

Again, we come back to technology as one of the culprits for the emotional crisis our children are facing. When most of us reading this grew up, there were certain unpleasant parts of life we were not exposed to until we were old enough to handle them. *But with the uncontrolled and often uncensored flow of information our young people are getting, especially through television and movies, they know too much too soon.*

By the time the average child has finished elementary school, he has watched 8,000 televised murders and 100,000 acts of violence. He knows all about sex, including that having it can kill. He is aware that many children his age are being physically abused or sexually molested, and that some children live on the streets because their parents cannot find a job.

Last year a friend of mine told me the following story. She and her husband were making love one evening, and the next morning, her five-year-old daughter approached her at the breakfast table.

"Mommy, last night I heard you and Daddy making noises in the bedroom, " she said with certainty. "What were you doing?"

My friend, her mother, thought carefully for a moment, and then answered:

"Honey, you know when you are eating something you really like, and you're happy, so you make a noise like 'Mmm-mmmmm'? Well, Daddy and I were really happy, so we were making happy noises."

Her daughter seemed to accept this explanation, and my friend breathed a sigh of relief. But it was short-lived. That afternoon, her little girl burst into the kitchen after being dropped off from school.

"Mommy, you told a fib!" she said accusingly. "You weren't making happy noises like I do. **You were having an orgasm!**"

My friend was speechless. Obviously her daughter had gone to school, asked around to her other five-year-old friends, and discovered the truth. As her mother shared this incident with me, we commiserated about the fact that when we were growing up, we weren't even sure what orgasms were until well into our teens.

I often witness parents of small children sharing stories similar to this, and everyone responds by saying "Isn't that cute?" or "Boy, the kids these days!!" But when I listen to what's underneath the laughter, I hear nervous panic. **"How can I possibly protect my child from hurt and harm,"** the **parents secretly question, "when they have already lost their innocence?"**

The answer is *"You cannot protect them,"* and this is what has all of us, whether we have children or not, so frightened for the next generation. The rates of teen pregnancy, drug and alcohol abuse, and juvenile crime among American young people are the highest in the world. In fact, much of the random violence that has made us feel like prisoners in our own homes is caused by kids with guns. Like their parents, our children feel powerless and full of rage, and many of them aren't as good at repressing those feelings as we are.

There is a principle in metaphysics that says *"We are what we perceive."* If our kids have been raised on a visual diet of violence, it should be no surprise that they are behaving violently. And we must understand that their violence, their attraction to irreverence, such as is expressed in the popular MTV cartoon *Beavis and Butt-head*, and the slightly dazed look in their clear eyes are all cries for help. They are lost in the trauma of our time, and it is up to us to help them, and ourselves, find a way out.

✦

"We must all go and work in the garden."
— VOLTAIRE

America, our beloved homeland, is in crisis. We can no longer ignore its cries for help. And yet, we cannot turn back the clock and undo the damage that has been done. Nor can we or should we turn totally away from the technology and materialism that has brought us to where we are. What, then, is the answer? How are we to heal our psychic wounds, and the wounds of our children? Where is our garden now, and how can we make it grow again?

We must rediscover those real moments of
love and connection that will give meaning
to our existence, no matter how crazy the
outside world becomes.

We must recommit to the compassion, caring,
and gratitude that have always been at the heart
of American values and, in this way,
reclaim our country's spirit.

We must bring our lives back into balance.

As treacherous as the present may appear to be, I am deeply hopeful about our future. For all around us there are very distinct signs that a healing has started to take place in America, both in our values and in the way we define success.

Oriental philosophy teaches us that nothing in the universe can swing too far in one direction without eventually seeking balance by swinging back. *We, as Americans, sense how out of balance we have gotten, and we're beginning to shift from a consciousness of self-indulgence to one of self-discovery.* We're turning back to religion and spiritual practices in great numbers. Whereas we once measured success in terms of status, wealth, and accomplishment, now we're beginning to measure it in terms of how happy we are, and how much peace of mind we've achieved.

Instead of believing that more of everything is better, we're returning to a *back to basics* philosophy. Our social trends all reflect this movement: We've gone from uncomfortable spike heels and impractical miniskirts to work boots and baggy dresses; we're trading in our fancy foreign cars for four-wheel drives and vans; we're exchanging complicated gourmet foods for mashed potatoes and meat loaf.

With our new love of anything that reminds us of less technological times, we are also turning away from the sophisticated and toward the simple—Western style dress, earthtoned colors in our clothing, and Native American jewelry are the latest fashion fads, cowboy movies and TV shows our new favorites, as if we're attempting to turn back the clock, to recapture our pioneer roots and the values that we lost along the way.

We are also rebuilding our nests and, thus, hoping to recreate some of the privacy our technology has taken from us. We're going out less and staying home more, not simply because we don't feel safe, but because we want to be alone. There is a strong trend toward privacy as we try to carve out the time to rediscover who we are and what we truly want.

✦

As we approach the twenty-first century, we, as Americans, are beginning to undergo a deep spiritual and emotional transformation. It is this transformation that is going to save us.

There is a wonderful quote attributed to a Chinese general who lived centuries ago:

> If the world is to be brought to order,
>   my nation must first be changed.
> If my nation is to be changed,
>   my hometown must be made over.
> If my hometown is to be reordered,
>   my family must first be set right.
> If my family is to be regenerated,
>   I, myself, must first be. . . .

Now, more than ever, we need real moments that will regenerate our tired souls and bring real meaning back into our lives. As our expectations continue to be diminished by economic realities, and as our outer lives continue to be limited by the constraints of time, space, and circumstances beyond our control, we must turn to the inner life, where there are no limits. There we will discover our true freedom, in the ability to find fulfillment *not* over the next hill, or in the next accomplishment, but right here, right now.

In this way, moment by moment, America will come back home. . . .

·3·

HIDING FROM
REAL MOMENTS

"In a seeker's search for wisdom, he spent three painful and grueling weeks climbing a tall, rocky mountain. At the peak, he found a wise, old guru and asked, 'Wise man, how might I make my life happier?'

"The Wise Man responded, 'To begin with, the next time you want to come up here, go to the other side of the mountain and take the tramway.'"

— GARY APPLE

In our lifelong search for happiness, many of us are making the journey a lot more difficult than it has to be: we are looking in the wrong direction for fulfillment; we are avoiding the very kinds of intimate experiences that will satisfy our hunger for purpose and meaning; *we are taking the long way up the mountain.*

This chapter will give you an opportunity to look at how you may be hiding from real moments, and how much time you waste in the process. If you read this with an open heart, I believe you will come to understand how you have been standing in your own way, and preventing yourself from experiencing the peace and fulfillment you deserve. And that's the first step toward discovering the real moments that are already there waiting for you.

✦

To begin, ask yourself these questions, and think carefully about the answers:

What makes me happy?
How often do I experience moments of true happiness?
How do I know when I am happy?

Don't be surprised if answering isn't as easy as you expect it should be:

> Often, we don't recognize real moments of happiness in our lives because we've been expecting something different—something bigger, flashier, and more dramatic.

To many of us, our pictures of how happiness should look and feel still have their roots in the "bigger must be better" mentality we were all brought up on. And so we have developed very unrealistic expectations of happiness—in our mind we see the word golden and glowing in capital letters: **HAPPINESS!!!!!!** The Big "H," the pie in the sky, the brass ring, the pot of gold at the end of the rainbow.

Thus, *we wait for happiness passively, as if it is something that will be bestowed on us at a particular time.* You just gave birth to your first child, and as you lie there exhausted from your labor, you think: "Now it's over and I should feel happy." You finally get the promotion you've been hoping for, and as you drive home to tell your wife, you think: "Now I can stop worrying about my job, and really be happy." You move into the new home you've dreamed of owning your whole life, and as you walk through each room, you think: "At last! My own home! Tonight I'll go to sleep happy."

But what if you don't? What if you feel good with a small "g," but not happy with a big "H"? "Something's wrong with me," you think suspiciously. "I *should* be feeling HAPPY, but I'm just happy." Or maybe you're not even feeling that— maybe you're actually feeling tired, or just O.K. Or maybe you're not feeling much of anything at all.

As we've seen, this is how we get hooked into believing that if we aren't feeling happy now, then happiness will surely be just around the next corner, or at the top of the next mountain. We know that big moment will come one day. On that day, you'll wake up and say . . . "Wait a minute . . . something feels different. Could it be? Could this be it? Oh my gosh, I think it is . . . I made it!! I'm finally happy!"

Waiting for Joy to Penetrate

I've spent much of my adult life working hard to try and be happy, and failing miserably at it. I could never understand what I was doing wrong, or why all the things I achieved and experienced weren't filling me up inside. One day about four years ago, I had an experience which gave me some of the answer. My husband and I had arrived at a small seaside town for a long-awaited vacation. We were exhausted from a year of long hours and very little free time, and I'd been counting the days until we got there.

The first two days passed quickly. Late one afternoon on the third day, I took a walk alone down a quiet road next to the ocean. The air was sweet and warm; the trees were filled with birds serenading the setting of the sun. And as I walked, I realized that I'd been feeling strange ever since our vacation started.

"What could possibly be bothering me?" I wondered. "It's perfect here. I'm swimming and sunbathing and making love and doing all the things I enjoy the most in the world. *I should be totally happy.*"

Then, it hit me. *I was waiting to be happy, as if happiness were some kind of condition that would descend upon me.* Like a child waiting anxiously for an expected surprise with her eyes closed, I was going through my days waiting for happiness to bang me over the head and announce its arrival. I'd wake up each morning and check . . . Am I happy yet? A little ache in my heart would respond: "No . . . not yet . . . check back later." And I'd go through my day, and periodically stop, as if to catch myself off guard, and think: "O.K.—how about now? Do I feel happy now?" Of course, the answer would always be "NO."

As I stood there on that beautiful road, a phrase appeared in my mind: "**Waiting for joy to penetrate.**" I realized that was exactly what I was doing. I was waiting for joy to penetrate my discontent, waiting for joy to make itself known. It's as if I wanted God to come down and announce: "Barbara De Angelis—Congratulations!! You are now officially happy! Enjoy it while it lasts."

I had happiness set up as being something *out of my control,* something that would or would not happen *to* me. When I went on vacation, I'd be happy. When I was relaxed, then I'd be happy. When I got a great tan, then I'd be happy. Of course, this meant that if I didn't go on the trip, or if I went and it rained for a week, then I wouldn't be happy, because those conditions I'd set up wouldn't be met.

So here I was, standing alone on a summer afternoon, waiting for happiness to announce its arrival in my life. And in that moment, I knew if I kept living as I did, I would have to wait forever.

I was waiting for happiness to come from the
outside into me, instead of creating it.
from the inside out.

I said in the beginning of this book that happiness is a skill,
not an acquisition. *It is a choice you make in each moment
about how you experience that moment, not a state you one day
achieve.* By waiting for Joy with a capital "J" to penetrate me,
I wasn't even recognizing the many real and happy moments
that were available.

This, then, is the first way we hide from real moments—**we
live in such a way that they are hidden from us.**

The Truth about Happiness

I believe that most people share a common and deadly misunderstanding about happiness—that is a fixed *state* we get
to, like turning forty, or becoming engaged, or being in recovery from an addiction. I'm forty, I'm engaged, I'm in recovery,
I'm happy. The truth, as I realized that day on my island walk,
is quite different:

Happiness is not a state of being—it is a
series of real moments.

These moments don't just happen to us. We need to create
opportunities for them to occur. *We need to stop hiding out
from those very experiences that will bring us, from the inside,
the experience of joy we're longing for.*

If happiness is not a state of being, that means *we cannot
always be happy.* For those of us brought up in the "we can
have it all" years, this is very disappointing news. I have seen
myself and my contemporaries struggle against this reality,
treating moments of pain, confusion, or unpleasantness of

any kind like mud we've stepped in and can't wait to wash off. Anything that doesn't feel good we try to avoid, and if we can't, we attempt to rush through these undesirable experiences as quickly as possible, and get back to "normal."

I once heard someone from another country say "**The trouble with Americans is that they expect to live with ongoing euphoria.**" I can't say that I disagree. We are so enamored with perfection that we often have a difficult time dealing with dualism—good and bad, success and setback, joy and sorrow.

I've probably been more guilty of this attitude than most people. Until six years ago, I used to misinterpret pain or sadness as a sign of my own spiritual failure. I believed that *if I were truly living a good life, I would always be happy, and since I was not happy, I must be doing something wrong.* This belief caused me to live with a lot of denial. For instance, I felt that I should always be happy in a relationship, so I avoided facing problems, confronting controversial issues, or even admitting to myself that I was unhappy. And I missed a lot of real moments, because although they were powerful or meaningful moments, they were not particularly happy moments, and I ran from them.

If we want to find peace and live with authenticity, there is a truth we must face—**pain, sadness, unpleasantness, are an integral part of life**, and will inevitably occur from time to time. We cannot *always* be happy. Carl Jung said it this way:

> "*There are as many nights as days, and the one is just as long as the other in the year's course. Even a happy life cannot be without a measure of darkness, and the word 'happy' would lose its meaning if it were not balanced by sadness.*"

Imagine that your child is ill, and you sit by her bedside late at night stroking her hair, soothing her frightened cries, waiting for her fever to go down. As you keep your watchful vigil, she is all that is important in the world, and nothing else seems to exist. You love her so much that it hurts, and the bond between you feels sacred. Are you happy? Of course not, but you can feel something deeply moving and meaningful about this experience, and you are right: *You are having a real moment.*

At the end of our time on earth, if we have lived fully, we will not be able to say: "I was always happy." Hopefully we will be able to say: "I have experienced a lifetime of real moments, and many of them were happy moments."

In this way, it is only in learning how to experience real moments, *one by one,* that we will also be able to experience happy moments.

Symptoms of Not Having Enough Real Moments

Most people I know have a "real moment deficiency." They aren't experiencing enough real moments in their lives, and when we are deficient in real moments, we end up being deficient in peace, contentment, and joy. When dogs have a mineral deficiency, they start eating the dirt in the yard to fulfill their craving for minerals. When your body has a deficiency of energy because you haven't eaten for a while, you start craving a candy bar or something sweet to help you get your blood sugar back up. **In this way, when we have a real moment deficiency, we develop unhealthy cravings and behaviors in an attempt to fill up our spiritual and emotional emptiness in other ways.**

Here are some symptoms that suggest you may not have enough real moments in your life:

✦ You need to constantly be doing something.

When you aren't experiencing enough real moments, you live with a gnawing sense of restlessness and dissatisfaction that will not go away. The only relief you get will be when you are busy doing something, because you are focused on your task on the outside, and not on what you're feeling inside. You might become a workaholic, spending twelve or fourteen hours a day on your career, never unwinding long enough to forget about work. "I'd love to take some time off," you proclaim, "but this project is taking longer than I thought." Of course, it always will, because you set it up that way. If you're a woman, you might become a rescuer or professional giver, spending all your time helping your friends, your family, the local charity, or whoever needs you. "I don't know how I got so busy!" you complain. The answer is simple: *You didn't say no to anyone or anything.*

When you have a need to be constantly doing something, you will always be able to find someone to help, or a new project to take on, and despite your protestations about wanting more time to enjoy your life, you will not make the time. The problem is that you will get approval and accolades for your addiction to activity, especially if you end up achieving a lot for yourself or contributing a lot to others, and this reinforces your tendency toward overdoing.

People who do too much get very nervous when they aren't focused on doing something. *They are uncomfortable with a void, and feel the need to fill it as quickly as possible.* They're the ones who vacuum their house twice a day, or make lists about what lists they need to make. They don't do well doing nothing on unstructured, quiet vacations. Instead, they make sure to see every museum or every tourist attraction or read five books. If you fall into this category, you probably have your TV or radio on most of the time when you are home to fill up the silence.

Doing too much inevitably turns into a vicious cycle.
Here's how it works:

You don't have enough real moments, so you feel
empty → You feel compelled to fill up your emptiness by always doing → When you are always doing, you have no free
time just to be → Since you have no free time, you don't
experience any real moments → You feel compelled to fill up
your emptiness by doing.

And the cycle goes on and on.

*There is only one way to break the cycle, and that is to stop
always doing, and create opportunities for the magic of real moments to occur:* At night after the kids are asleep, turn off the
television, sit quietly with the person you love and have a real
moment of intimate connection; instead of scheduling every
moment of your Saturday morning with errands, put aside
twenty minutes to take a walk in the park and see what real
moments with Nature you encounter; the next time you get
together with friends, don't plan to do anything in particular—spend some time just being in each other's presence and
enjoying the real moments that result.

Leave room in your life for real moments by having times
when you aren't *doing* anything.

✦ *You have an addiction.*

All addictions have one thing in common—they numb
you out to what is happening in the moment. They offer,
instead, an intense sensory experience which either absorbs
all of your attention or distorts reality. You may think you're
having a real moment, but you are not, because your addictive
activity, such as drinking or doing drugs, is actually disconnecting you from your true emotions and, therefore, making
it difficult for you to connect with others around you.

People who are hungry for more real moments
often use addictions to get a temporary
hit of happiness.

But because the feeling of happiness that addictions provide
is caused by the substance or behavior, and therefore is always
temporary, you can't feel good without it. This is how you get
hooked into wanting and needing more.

Addictions are so socially acceptable in America that, often,
people don't even realize that they have one. I'm not talking
about addictions to hard drugs like heroin or cocaine—those
we have judgments about. It's the tolerated addictions—
alcohol, cigarettes, recreational drugs like marijuana, tran-
quilizers and painkillers, gambling, pornography—that are so
insidious, and in this way, so deadly, because we don't think
of them as addictions at all. We call them *"habits."*

America has a real double standard about which "habits"
we call serious addictions, and which "habits" we don't. Dad
stands before his sixteen-year-old, waving his nightly martini
in his hand as he berates his son for being a "pothead." A
congressman sits puffing away on his fortieth cigarette of the
day as he deplores the drug dealers who are ruining the youth
of this country. Mom screams at her daughter for trying psy-
chedelic mushrooms at a rock concert, and then retreats to
her room to take a tranquilizer so she can sleep.

Whether it's full-blown alcoholism or watching TV ten
hours a day, *regular use of addictive substances, or regular in-
dulgence in addictive behavior robs you of your ability to fully
feel*. Do whatever it takes and get whatever help you need to
stop, and try getting high on living.

✦ You are cynical, pessimistic, and sarcastic.

I have great compassion for cynical people, because I know
that underneath their armor of sarcasm and disdain, they are
hungry for more real moments in their lives.

When we don't experience real moments, we
will have difficulty seeing the purpose and
meaning of our existence.

Without a sense of meaning, life is simply a series of random
events as we move purposelessly through each day. And when
we see no purpose, no sense to the way things are, it is easy
to become cynical and to stop caring.

Cynicism is a cover-up for pain, *an expression of angry
hopelessness that the world is the way it is. Cynics are often
frustrated believers who feel deep disappointment in people and
in life itself.* Think of someone you know who appears to have
a negative or pessimistic attitude. When you look into their
eyes, you will see a wounded spirit.

If you have lost your faith in why we are here and what
we are supposed to be doing, you aren't having enough real
moments. It is these moments that themselves will bring
meaning back into your life and make it all worthwhile.

✦ *You live your life through others.*

A grandmother sits alone in her apartment, watching soap
operas and talk shows all day long. She glances at the phone,
wondering if her granddaughter will call later tonight. She's
happy when she hears from her granddaughter—in fact she
lives for the calls and the occasional visits. She thinks back to
Thanksgiving when her granddaughter came to stay for three
days, and she smiles. Checking her watch, she realizes that
there are only four more hours until she should be getting
home from work. "Maybe I'll call her tonight," she decides.
"It's been a pretty uneventful week."

If your greatest joy in the past few years has been the
success and happiness of your children or grandchildren, or
your mate, you are not having enough real moments in your

life. You are living your life through someone else. I'm not talking about feeling happy with and proud of those you love. I'm talking about making other people the center of your life, and not having one of your own.

I have seen mothers do this with their children, rejoicing when a child succeeds, mourning when a child fails, becoming so enmeshed in their offspring that they are utterly dependent on their sons and daughters for validation. I have seen grandparents do this with their grandchildren, turning them into their only source of love, making seeing or talking to them their only purpose for living. I've seen wives do this with their husbands, losing their identity completely, gaining a sense of self-worth only through their husbands' accomplishments or their husbands' status in the community.

When we have lost a sense of our own purpose in life, we often latch on to someone else's purpose as a replacement. But it is never too late to find your own purpose again—in fact, knowing your own purpose is what will keep you alive longer.

No matter what age you are, or what your circumstances might be, you are special, and still have something unique to offer. Your life, because of who *you* are, has meaning.

If you feel guilty reading this, perhaps it's time to take your life back, to release those you love from feeling you are living through them, and to rediscover your special purpose by having more real moments. You have your own special gifts to give, whether through volunteering your time at a retirement home or hospital, becoming a foster grandparent to a child who has little or no family, or helping out at a local day-care facility. *You do make a difference.*

✦ *You are judgmental.*

By definition, judging means *standing outside* of a situation, or a relationship, and criticizing what you see. You watch someone at work making mistakes and think "What a space case he is!" You feel frustrated driving behind an elderly person who's going fifteen miles an hour and think "How can they give licenses to these people?"

You can't be judgmental and have a real moment at the same time.

In order to have a real moment, you need to be totally in a situation, fully feeling it from the inside out. You need to be connected with the person you're with or the environment you're in. *When you are judgmental, you are disconnecting from that person or experience, thus making it impossible for you to have a real moment at that particular time.*

W hen you let go of your judgments and create
a moment of connection with another person,
you take the first step toward being truly
compassionate.

Here are two stories about how I learned to stop hiding from real moments, and learned some powerful lessons in compassion:

Learning Compassion on a Street Corner

Last year I decided to buy a new car, and set aside time one afternoon to visit a local car dealership. When I arrived at the lot, a salesman about fifty-five years old agreed to take me for a test drive in a car I was thinking about purchasing. Five minutes passed, ten minutes passed—he was still trying to find the keys, and I started getting annoyed. Things got worse when he couldn't remember a special alarm code used to unlock the car, and had to go back inside and look it up in a file. Now I was feeling incredibly tense, and resentful that he was wasting so much time. Finally, we got into the car and drove off the lot. But we'd only gone one mile from the showroom when the car stopped dead in the middle of the street.

"What happened?" I asked. "Did I do something wrong?"

"No," the perplexed salesman replied. "Maybe it just wasn't warmed up enough."

Then, I noticed the gas gauge was on empty. "Sir," I said in a frosty voice, "there is no gas in this car."

"Oh gee, you're right. I guess the mechanic forgot to fill it up."

Now I was fuming. I was going to be late for a meeting, and here we were stuck in the middle of a busy intersection, causing a traffic jam.

The salesman went into a nearby store to call the dealership and ask them to pick us up, and left me standing on the street corner. I was furious, and totally frustrated that I'd picked such an idiot to sell me a car. "What a moron," I cursed to myself. "Here I am wasting my whole afternoon because he wasn't smart enough to check and see if the car had gas. This guy has no brains!"

Ten minutes later, the embarrassed-looking salesman came out to wait with me. It was a very warm day in Los Angeles. His face was beet red, his shirt was drenched with sweat, and I started getting nervous that he was going to have a stroke. Taking pity on him, I decided to strike up a conversation.

"I didn't mean to seem rude earlier," I began, "it's just that I'm in a hurry to get to an appointment, and now my schedule is all messed up."

"Please don't apologize," he responded in a quiet voice. "It's all my fault. I'm having a horrible day—some personal problems—my mind just isn't working."

In that moment, I realized I had a choice. I could continue to judge him, which felt horrible to both of us. Or I could connect with him from the heart. And that's what I did.

"I'm sorry to hear you're having some problems," I said. "I know how distracted I am when I'm upset about something important."

That was all he needed to hear to feel safe. "It's my mother," he blurted out. *"I just got a call from the hospital—they were doing exploratory surgery and found out she has terminal cancer.* It's spread all over her body. After work, I have to tell her the bad news, and I don't know if I can handle it."

Tears welled up in my eyes as I felt this man's sadness. No wonder he'd been so distracted. No wonder he couldn't concentrate on selling me a car. Suddenly, running out of gas, being late to my appointment, and everything else seemed totally insignificant. Because I'd been willing to have a real moment with the salesman, I now understood his behavior, felt his grief, and was given a wonderful reminder that, to paraphrase a Native American aphorism, *we should never judge another human being until we've walked a mile in his or her moccasins.*

Seeing the Ghost of My Grandfather at the Wheel

Oddly enough, the second compassion lesson also has to do with an automobile. Several months ago, I was on my way to an important meeting when I found myself driving behind a car going about twenty miles an hour in a forty-five-mile-an-hour zone. There was no way to pass this car, so I was stuck following it as it puttered along, block by block. I tried honking my horn, hoping the person in the car would get the message, but it didn't help. As each moment passed, I became more and more agitated.

Finally, I caught a peek at the driver, and discovered it was an elderly man who looked about eighty years old. "I should have known," I thought bitterly. "Some old guy who shouldn't even have a license anymore." I was about to start honking my horn again at this hazardous slowpoke when suddenly and unexpectedly, my mind flashed on my grandfather, who'd died when I was nineteen. I loved my grandfather so much, and had been devastated when he passed away. I remembered how frail he'd been in his later years, his body betraying him with prostate cancer, his face creased with pain. I recalled how difficult it had been for him, having spent his whole life giving unselfishly to others, to face his failing health, and have to rely on friends, family, and strangers to take care of him.

Overcome with memories, my eyes filled with tears and my heart flooded with new compassion. I realized that the elderly driver of that car might as well have been my grandfather, and was probably somebody else's. He wasn't driving slowly in order to annoy me. In his last years, he was out taking a drive, savoring another day of life.

I watched the car moving carefully along in front of me, and silently apologized to the driver in my heart: "Please forgive me for becoming so angry with you, dear old man," I thought. "I'm glad you're still alive today, and I know that driving on your own might be one of the very last freedoms you have left. And forgive me for being so impatient with your pace and pressuring you to go faster. I now know that you're going as fast as you can. . . ."

I eased my foot off the accelerator, and allowed myself to tune in to the slow rhythms of the driver in front of me, respecting them, celebrating them. Finally he put on his blinker to make a turn, and as he disappeared around the corner, I help up a hand and waved in his direction. "Good-bye, Grand-Pop," I whispered. "Thank you for the reminder. . . . I miss you."

✦

Both of these events were precious, real moments in my life. *Each was unexpected, unplanned, and only existed because I was willing to stop and pay attention to what was really happening.* I could have hidden from the moment by criticizing the people involved, or condemning the circumstances. Instead, I followed the quiet impulses of my heart and *felt the moment rather than judged it.* In doing so, both times I received powerful gifts and necessary reminders.

> When you learn how to stop hiding from real
> moments you'll find that they are happening
> all around you, and can offer themselves
> when you least expect it.

How and Why We Avoid Real Moments

The first step in beginning to create more real moments in your life is recognizing how and why you avoid them.

✦ *We avoid real moments by being too busy or distracted to pay attention.*

Most of us frequently do two or three things at once. You're talking on the phone to your friend, paying your bills, and watching TV, all at the same time. How can you possibly have a moment of true connection and meaning with your friend? You can't. So you don't.

Watch yourself for the rest of today, or tomorrow. Notice how often you are focusing on several activities, but not fully enjoying or experiencing one of them. Maybe you're driving to work, listening to the radio, and thinking about an important project all at once. You're not really driving, listening, or thinking at all. You're not fully doing anything. So you miss the drive, you miss enjoying the music, and you miss getting deep insights into your project. And you definitely miss real moments.

✦

When I go from my home to my office, I drive down a long, wide road that starts out at the top of a hill, and ends up right at the coast highway next to the ocean. There's a traffic light at the bottom of this hill that's notorious for being very long—if you aren't lucky enough to get through it as you're coming down the hill, you can sit there at the light for six or seven minutes, waiting for it to change.

One day, soon after I decided to write this book, I was cruising down the hill, hoping to make the light, and just as the car in front of me passed through the intersection, the light turned red. I sat in my car and thought about how much I hated getting stuck here all the time, staring at the signal as if that would speed up the process. I looked anxiously at the clock every minute to see how much time had passed, and worried about all the things I had to accomplish that day.

All of a sudden, I was struck by the absurdity of the situation: Here I was, looking out on a beautiful sandy beach and beyond that, the ocean. The sun was shining in a perfectly clear sky, and the light shimmered on the water. *Millions of people traveled from all around the world every year to visit this very spot, and to look at this spectacular view that I wasn't even noticing or enjoying because I was too distracted and too much in a hurry!!*

I realized then that this was how I was living most of my life, doing so much of everything that I wasn't paying complete attention to anything. The stoplight was just a reflection of how few of my experiences, whether waiting at a light, having a conversation, or listening to music, I actually experienced. No wonder I'd decided to write a book called *Real Moments*—I needed to read it myself!!

I'd always considered having to stop at that intersection a nuisance. Now, I decided it was God's way of slowing me down when I was going too fast, and reminding me to pay attention:

"Stop . . . breathe in the fresh air . . . look at the ocean . . . it looks like it goes on forever, doesn't it? Isn't this a beautiful planet you live on? How lucky you are to drive by this lovely stretch of beach every day! How fortunate you are to be alive!!!! . . . Feel better? . . . Good . . . O.K., I'll change the light now. . . . Have a wonderful morning!!"

That day, I had a revelation at that intersection, and by the time the light finally changed, so had I. **By paying attention to the fact that I wasn't paying attention, I'd experienced a real moment that transformed the way I lived my life.** Now, each time I am met with a red light at the bottom of the hill, I smile and say "Thank you . . . I must have needed to stop and enjoy the view."

✦

Sometimes we avoid real moments because we are afraid of them. *We don't pay attention because, in the secret places of our heart, we suspect that by paying attention, we will discover some unpleasant truths about ourselves or our life.* This suspicion is correct:

Real moments can be very confrontational.
When you stop doing too much and take time to
have real moments by paying attention, you will,
undoubtedly, come face-to-face with emotions,
revelations, or realities you weren't aware of.

Many years ago, I was in a very unfulfilling and incompatible relationship. I loved this man very much, but we were not right for each other, a fact I'd been trying to ignore because I didn't want the relationship to end. And so I filled my life with so much activity, so many projects, that I was literally working every day and evening, every weekend, and even on holidays. My work brought me tremendous satisfaction, and, unconsciously, I avoided paying attention to the relationship.

The time came for us to take a vacation, and for some reason, I decided not to bring any work with me. We had booked a room on a tiny island in the middle of nowhere, and for the first time since we met, we would be alone with no distractions, no agendas, no business to discuss. I remember getting on the plane with a hard knot in my stomach, not understanding why I felt so anxious. But I soon found out.

The second day of our trip, I spent an afternoon by myself on a deserted beach. It was a whole afternoon of real moments during which I could no longer escape from the truth in my heart—*I needed to end this relationship.* Until now, I had successfully avoided confronting the truth because I was so afraid of the pain it was going to cause him, and the drama it would create in my life. But there, on that island, there was nowhere and no way for me to hide from my feelings anymore.

It took me several weeks to get up the courage to tell the man I loved that I was leaving, but finally, I did. I often wonder what would have happened to us if I had not taken the time to experience some real moments with myself, if I had not faced the fear of confronting my truth. How much longer would we have lived together, not getting what we wanted and needed? We are both happily married to other people now, and have found out where we truly belong.

Sometimes, it does take courage to have a real moment, and to be open to whatever it reveals to you. But the alternative is avoidance, denial, and a life spent running from yourself. . . .

"What you bring forth out of yourself from the inside will save you. What you do not bring forth out of yourself from the inside will destroy you."

—GOSPEL OF THOMAS

✦

Later in this book, I'll share some techniques for creating real moments, but for now, just try an experiment—*Sometime in the next few days, do one activity with complete attention, and without distracting yourself.* It could be driving in your car and really paying attention to what you see around you, or preparing dinner and really paying attention to the fact that you are preparing nourishment for the people you love.

I tried this recently on an airplane. I decided to really experience flying in the plane for the full four hours my flight took, not to read a book or watch a movie, but to be in a speeding metal tube 35,000 feet up in the air. And that's just what I did. I sat next to a window and watched the earth pass beneath me for four hours straight. I witnessed tributaries turning into large rivers, plains bursting forth into mountains, and then sinking down into plains again. I saw small cities, large cities, and tiny towns, all looking so gentle from the sky. By the time we landed, I felt a love for the land of our country that I'd never experienced before, and I walked off that plane filled with peace.

✦ We avoid real moments by putting up boundaries between ourselves and other people.

Many of my most loving real moments have occurred when I was experiencing a connection with someone else—my husband, my dog Bijou, a close friend, and often, people I'm just meeting for the first time. What creates a real moment between two people? *Intimacy.*

Intimacy occurs when the boundaries between
you and someone else melt, and
your hearts touch.

If you have a problem with intimacy, and many of us do, you aren't going to be eager to create real moments with people in your life. You won't feel safe, because during real moments, your usual boundaries are penetrated. Your innermost feelings are revealed, leaving you feeling vulnerable, unprotected. *And if in the past, you allowed someone to get close to you, and it caused you pain, you won't find it easy to be intimate again without experiencing a lot of fear.*

This is one of the most common ways we hide from real moments—we give in to fear, and decide to avoid or resist intimacy. You become an expert at putting up emotional walls, psychic barricades around your heart. The walls keep out pain, but they also make it difficult for you to have real moments: since other people's love can't get in and your love can't get out, you don't experience intimacy. The boundaries that are there to protect you become an emotional prison, insulating you from the very moments of communion you need to be happy.

Magical Connections and Blessed Encounters

If you want to experience more real moments of intimacy in your life, you don't have to wait until you get into a relationship or marry. After all, we share this world with over five billion people. Unfortunately, we have so many rules about whom we can connect with, when connection is appropriate, and how much we should connect that we miss many opportunities for what I call *"magical connections and blessed encounters."*

In our society, we call people we don't know "strangers,"

and we go out of our way to avoid connecting with them.
When you bump into someone in an elevator, you immediately apologize, as if you've done something wrong. When
you notice someone looking at you for a while at a restaurant,
you immediately assume either you have a run in your panty
hose, or a stain on your tie, that the person is trying to pick
you up, or that they're a psychopathic stalker and you're the
next victim. Very rarely do you think, "Oh, there's another
human being looking at me and making contact."

According to our "Boundary Book," there are certain "acceptable" subjects one can discuss with strangers: the
weather, sports, entertainment, gossip. You can always complain with a stranger, since both of you simultaneously judging something else makes you feel safe with one another. And
as long as each party respects the boundaries, you're comfortable. But none of these conversations will help you experience
a real moment together.

If you're willing to share a real moment, you can learn
things about yourself from strangers that you often can't learn
from people you are close with.

> Strangers can be very pure mirrors of truth,
> reflecting back to you whatever you've been
> needing to see, delivering cosmic messages
> you've been needing to hear.

There is a safety in anonymity that allows us, when we
don't know someone, to pierce through layers of ego and ex-
pectation, and open up to truths which are waiting to reveal
themselves. I have had many spectacular real moments with
strangers—while waiting in lines, meeting in a store, and especially on airplanes, since I travel so much. Let me share one
with you. . . .

How I Met My Mirror in the Sky

I was tired when I boarded the plane in San Francisco that would carry me home to Los Angeles. I'd just finished two days of speeches and TV appearances, and felt talked out. So I was really looking forward to the flight, and planned to meditate and sleep the whole way—that is, until I got to my assigned row, and saw a little girl about nine years old squirming around in the seat next to me. "Oh no," I groaned inwardly, "not a child—I don't have the energy for it. Please let her be in the wrong seat." But I was out of luck. She was in the right place, and so was I.

I sat down and began strategizing about how I could avoid talking with her. "Maybe if I just close my eyes, she'll be afraid to say anything," I thought. "Or perhaps I should ask the flight attendant to find me a different seat." As we taxied down the runway, I was already counting the minutes until the flight was over.

All at once, I realized how unconsciously I was behaving. "Pay attention . . ." my inner voice reminded me. Throughout my lifetime, I'd learned over and over again that *there are no accidents in the Universe*—I'd been placed next to this little girl for a reason. If I was having such a strong negative reaction to the experience, there was probably a powerful lesson in it for me somewhere.

And so, I introduced myself to Bethany, who appeared to have been waiting for me to reach out to her. Once she saw that I was truly interested, Bethany shared herself without reservation. She began by telling me that she was very excited because this was her first flight in an airplane, and she was flying to meet her father in Los Angeles. Her parents had recently divorced, and her dad moved away with her brother and sister. Bethany was also given the choice of being with the rest of her family, but she chose to stay with her mother.

"That must have been a difficult decision," I told her, "to know you wouldn't be with everyone else."

"It was, but I felt like Mom needed me," Bethany explained with great solemnity. "She's going through a hard time." She went on to explain that her mother married and had kids at a young age, and was now feeling trapped and tied down. "She has lots of boyfriends, and goes out all the time," Bethany told me in a confidential tone, "and I don't like it because I'm alone so much."

"I'll bet you miss your dad a lot," I offered. Bethany's eyes filled with tears.

"I really miss him, and everyone else too. He calls me every day to see if I'm O.K."

"And what do you tell him?"

"I tell him I'm fine, but sometimes I'm not. . . ."

My heart hurt as I saw the pain and confusion in Bethany's bright eyes, too much pain for a nine-year-old to be carrying around. She was wise beyond her years . . . she had to be. And I saw the whole picture—Mom starts running around; Dad files for and gets custody of the kids, because Mom is unfit. But compassionate, loving Bethany doesn't want to abandon Mom. So she gives up a stable new life, the protection of her father and growing up with her brother and sister, to make sure Mom knows that someone still loves her. And night after night, she sits alone or with a baby-sitter, watching TV, waiting for Mom to come home from a hot date, and coping with her loneliness by convincing herself that she'd done the right thing.

And so we talked, Bethany and me. I told her about my own parents' divorce when I was eleven, how torn I felt trying to take sides, how I felt damaged and different because I didn't have a normal family like all my friends, and how I used to cry myself to sleep. "Me too!" she chimed in. I explained what I'd learned once I grew up about how parents are just people, and that inside of them, they are still little kids just like her. I tried to give her insight into why her mom was doing the things she was, and that just because she was the mom and Bethany the child, it didn't mean Bethany might not see things Mom didn't see. I suggested that she tell her dad how unhappy she was, and not worry that she'd make him feel guilty, because he needed to know. I reminded her that, above all, she needed to take care of herself first, even if it meant moving away. And then I told her how hard I'd worked to love myself, to know my parents' divorce had nothing to do with me, and to accomplish good things in my life.

"Look at what I've done as a grown-up," I said proudly, showing her several of the books I'd written which I happened to have in my briefcase.

"Wow—is this really you?" she asked, wide-eyed.

"Honest, it's me. And I've even been on television."

Bethany almost jumped out of her seat. "Wait a minute . . . wait a minute . . ." she exploded. "I"VE SEEN YOU!!!! IT WAS ON SOME TALK SHOW, LIKE *OPRAH* OR *GERALDO*, RIGHT?!!!"

"Right."

"Oh my God, Oh my God, I am so excited!!!" Bethany began bouncing up and down.

"Do you know why I'm telling you all this? *So that you always remember that it doesn't matter where you came from—it just matters where you're going.* You're a very special, smart and talented person, Bethany. You can be anything you want to be. Hey, if I can do it, so can you."

Our flight was almost over. Bethany and I exchanged phone numbers, and I promised to send some books for her mother and father, and a special surprise just for her. She was quiet now, her face pressed against the window, enchanted by the scenery beneath her.

Suddenly, I got it. How could I not have seen the truth

sooner? **Bethany was *me*.** I had just spent an hour in an airplane talking to myself as a nine-year-old child, telling her all the things I wished someone had told me when I was in so much pain, showing her a vision of who she was destined to become someday, sharing lessons it took me thirty years to figure out. *God had placed me in a seat next to Little Barbara, with a different set of circumstances and a different name, but with the same troubled spirit, so I could heal that old wounded part of me.*

With Bethany as my mirror, I saw that, indeed, I had triumphed over my past, that I could forgive it even more than I had done before, and that part of my purpose was to share the lessons of my journey with all the big and little Barbaras and Bethanys and Bobs of the world. I shook my head, marveling at the perfection of the moment. Bethany had been my teacher in the sky as much as I had been hers, delivering a message I was meant to have, just as I delivered one to her. We were true sisters in spirit.

Just then, Bethany turned to me, and I saw her eyes were filled with tears.

"What's wrong?" I asked.

"Nothing—it's just that this is the happiest day of my life."

"Why, because you got to fly in a plane and you're going to see your dad in a few minutes?"

Bethany looked straight into my soul, and with a radiant smile she answered:

"No, because I met you . . ."

No honor, no award, no standing ovation I've ever received meant more to me than what Bethany said that afternoon. She rendered me speechless (not an easy task!). We've kept in touch, and the last I heard, she was still living with her mom, but her dad had moved back to be near her.

I will never forget Bethany. She gave me one of the most profound and healing real moments of my life. Soon after our meeting, as promised, I sent her a teddy bear so she could have a special friend to share her feelings and secrets with.

When I found out she named it Barbara, I cried. . . .

✦

"Just think how happy you'd be if you lost everything you have right now—and then, got it back again. . . ."
— ANONYMOUS

I hope you are having a real moment reading this. . . .

I hope I am helping you pay attention to forces and feelings inside you that you've been hiding from. . . .

I hope I'm getting through the layers of forgetfulness you've collected through the years, and that you're starting to re-member why you are really here. . . .

I'm telling you all of this because I don't want you to waste any more time. You may not be aware that you are wasting time. In fact, your life might feel like you're squeezing forty hours of work and responsibility into a twenty-four-hour day. The time I'm speaking about that gets wasted is the time you don't spend in each moment, experiencing and appreciating it for what it is, the time that you lose because you live through it unmindfully, throwing away the opportunity for love, for connection, for learning, as if you have all the time in the world.

Several months ago I received a tearful phone call from a friend, informing me that she'd just been diagnosed with can-cer. We spoke for a while, but even after I hung up, I couldn't get her off my mind. That evening, as my husband and I lay in bed, I told him the unfortunate news, and shared the strong emotions that had been coming up for me all day. I'd been thinking about my friend, who was my age, and how she must have been feeling that night, alone, except for her cats, in her dark bedroom. I knew that if I were she, I'd be wondering how much time I had left to live, and how I should spend that time if my cancer was not cured.

"How would I change my life if I found out I was dying?" I wondered aloud to my husband.

"I guess that would depend on how many years the doctors estimated you had left," Jeffrey said.

"I know one thing, I wouldn't waste even one day not fully feeling and enjoying every moment of life."

Suddenly, I was seized with a searing truth. Like my friend, I *too was dying,* perhaps not today or tomorrow, but thirty or forty or fifty years in the not-so-distant future:

Why would I need to know I was about to lose everything to really enjoy it?

Why do so many of us only get motivated through fear and loss?

Why do we wait until we're ill to appreciate the miracle of our bodies?

Why do we wait until our partner is walking out the door to realize how much we need him or her?

Why do we put off living the way we want to live, as if we have all the time in the world?

Our time here on earth is so short. If we are fortunate, we have approximately 80 years, 29,200 days to experience life and all it offers. How many of us, as we breathe our last breath, will truly be able to say *"I feel fulfilled with who I was, and with what I did. I enjoyed all the moments God gave me"*?

Often, it is only those who are on death's doorstep that can see clearly enough to remind us of the precious gift each day of life truly is. The late actor and director, Michael Landon, shared this message in an interview just a few weeks before his death several years ago:

"While life lasts, it's good to remember that death is coming, and it's good that we don't know when. It keeps us alert. It reminds us to live

while we have the chance. Somebody should tell us that we are dying. Then we might live life to the limit, every minute of every day. Do it! Whatever you want to do, do it now. There are only so many tomorrows. . . ."

We need to stop wasting time hiding from real moments and, instead, seek them out, not next year, not when you finish reading this book, but NOW. And that is an easy thing to do. Because:

Real moments are always available.

We do not have to look far to find them.

. . . They are as close as the person sitting next to you in an airplane, or the waitress who brings you your coffee each morning before work, or the friend going through a difficult time who reaches out to you.

. . . They are there whenever and wherever you decide to pay attention to what's in front of you.

. . . They are blessed encounters and magical connections just waiting to happen, if only you will give them the chance.

Part Two

REAL MOMENTS
AND LIVING

· 4 ·

GIVING BIRTH
TO YOUR SELF

"Where am I? Who am I?
How did I come to be here?
What is this thing called the world?
How did I come into the world?
Why was I not consulted?
And If I am compelled to take part in it,
Where is the director?
I want to see him."

— SØREN KIERKEGAARD

In the process of living out the years of our lives, there comes a time when we realize that, somehow, we've gotten lost along the way. We've lost our own sense of purpose and direction. We've lost the ability to live by our own values and beliefs. We've lost our capacity for uninhibited joy and celebration. We move through each day with a buried uneasiness, a silent suspicion that something is not right. But no matter how hard we search for the source of our discomfort, we can find nothing apparently wrong. We are chasing a ghost who will not reveal himself.

We try doing more, going to new places, changing the way our bodies look, buying something different, or loving someone new, and perhaps for a while, we feel better. But then, the shadow of discontent returns, stronger than ever, and we begin to wonder if something is seriously wrong with us. Maybe this is the mid-life crisis we've heard about. Maybe we're just ungrateful for what we have, and will never be satisfied with anything. Maybe we're just not meant to be happy.

What are we looking for? **We are searching for the pieces of ourselves that we've lost, and without them, it is difficult to experience real moments.**

What happened to these pieces?

- ✦ Some of them were taken away by our parents or caretakers, in an attempt to turn us into what they thought we should be.
- ✦ Some of them we've given away to others in an attempt to be accepted or loved.
- ✦ Some of them we've hidden away, frightened of what others might think if they knew our secret selves.
- ✦ And some of them we've simply forgotten about, because we've been trying so hard to be something other than who we really are.

Without those pieces, we will never experience the wholeness we crave and the peace we are searching for. We will find it difficult to have the real moments we need. How do we get the pieces back? How do we return to a state of wholeness? We must pass from the cramped, yet familiar womb of who we have been into the person we are meant to be. We must take the journey from our old life of sacrifice and limitation into a new life of authenticity and freedom. **We must give birth to ourself again.**

"There came a time when the risk to remain tight in a bud was more painful than the risk it took to blossom."

—ANAÏS NIN

What we, in our country, have been calling a mid-life crisis is really a spiritual crisis. *If, by the time we reach an age at which we expected to feel content, whether it's thirty, forty, or beyond, we are not living with purpose, meaning, and many real moments, we will find ourselves dissatisfied and unfulfilled.* One day, we wake up and look at who we've become, and we don't like what we see. All of our hard work, all of our efforts have not given us the happiness and peace of mind we thought they would. The values and priorities we believed in have led us to an empty fulfillment. *"Is this all there is?"* we ask ourselves. This condition has been misinterpreted as everything from a fear of death, a yearning to be young again, or boredom with routine and predictability. But it is none of these. *It is a state of spiritual panic.*

What allows us, as human beings,
to psychologically survive life on earth,
with all of its pain, drama, challenges,
is a sense of purpose and meaning.

Purpose means that there is a reason for you to be here, that you have something to do that matters, *that your existence is significant.*

And meaning implies that your experience of living brings you fulfillment and joy from moment to moment, *that living your purpose is worth it.*

When you lose your sense of purpose and your experience of meaning, you lose those things that fuel your spirit, and enable it to make its presence known in your life. You become disconnected from an inner source of serenity, and feel compelled to search in vain for something or someone to fill the void. You're alive, but you're not fully living. You are missing out on real moments.

Maybe you are experiencing this right now. Maybe you've been feeling trapped in a life or a relationship that isn't giving you what you thought it would. Maybe you've worked for many years to get somewhere, and now that you've arrived, you aren't sure you want to be there in the first place. Maybe you think everything should be fine in your life, because you have what you've always wanted, but it doesn't feel fine. Maybe you've been feeling unsettled for a while, and haven't known what it was until this moment. Or maybe you're young, and suspect that if you don't stop and pay attention now, you'll end up in the same rut your parents did.

✦

Giving birth to yourself requires that you ask yourself difficult questions:

Who am I?

Am I living as the person I want to be?

What have I really been doing with my life?

Am I happy?

What brings me joy?

What do I need to let go of to be free?

These questions are the contractions in your rebirth process that will push you through to a new, liberated existence. Asking and answering them requires great emotional courage. It means seeing parts of yourself you've been ignoring, facing truths about your life you have been evading, confronting dreams you have been avoiding. Birth is never easy. But the reward for your having taken the journey will be life as you've never lived it before.

So if you, like me, are in the process of giving birth to yourself, know that this is a powerful and sacred time of your life. A force of transformation has seized hold of you. Like a strong wind at your back, it will help propel you in the direction you need to go. Surrender to its currents, and if you get a little frightened of the speed at which you're traveling, whatever you do, don't try to turn and go back the other way. There's no where to go but out. And as the poet Robert Frost said:

"The best way out is always through."

Where You Got Lost Along the Way

When did we first start to disconnect from who we really are? When did we give the first piece of ourselves away? It began the moment we were born. From the time we are small children, we collect other people's values and beliefs, and make them our own. It started with your parents. Through their words and actions, they demonstrated their values and traditions, and passed them on to you. You learned how to express or not express feelings, how to deal with conflict, how to treat those different from you, how to give affection, how to practice your spiritual beliefs, how to celebrate holidays and special occasions, how to bring up children, how to cook, what to cook, how to set the table, how to take vacations—the list goes on and on. You did not study formally—*you watched, listened, and learned.*

Most of us don't consciously choose to think, behave, love, walk, talk, or eat like our parents. It just happens, sometimes so subtly that we don't even notice the similarities until someone else points them out. "You're kidding!" we respond with disbelief. "But I'm so *different* from them." Maybe yes, maybe no. *It's how you are the same that's the issue.*

How We Abandoned Our Dreams

There is another way we lost ourselves: **We adopted our parents' or social group's hopes, dreams, and expectations, leaving little or, in some cases, no room for our own.** You became a doctor because your father was a doctor, and from the time you were little, it was just assumed you would be too. You still live in your hometown, and belong to the same church as your parents, just because no one in your family has ever left. You went to college and joined a sorority just like your mom did, and volunteered for the same causes, because that's what all the girls in your high school crowd did. You got married at twenty-three and had two children right away, because all your older brothers and sisters had families early.

Sometimes, taking the path others expect you to follow may truly coincide with your own dreams as well. But more often, it is a path that takes you far away from your vision, far away from the possibility of your own adventures, far away from yourself. *Years, even decades later, you wake up and face the fact that you did what others considered right or wanted you to do, not what you wanted to do.*

Maybe you became a doctor like your parents wanted you to be, but you've always dreamed of being an architect, and now, at forty-seven, you're burned out and miserable. Maybe you secretly longed to leave your hometown and move to the other side of the country, and now, years later, you've started a family and have no hopes of getting out. Maybe you didn't want to go to college at all, but wanted to study meditation and yoga, and now you find yourself living a life just like your mother's, married to the same kind of man, going to the same kinds of parties, with your spiritual self buried deep inside. And maybe you found the husband and had the kids right away because that was the thing to do, and now you're only thirty and you feel like your husband is a stranger, your children are a burden, and you dream of running away from them all.

As long as you have not reexamined your belief systems, and discarded the portions you never actually choose as an adult, you will never fully grow up.

Taking on the values of others affects our relationships, our personal philosophy, our work ethic, the way we raise our children, and the way we treat ourselves. No wonder so many of us feel something is not right with our lives: Our authentic self is covered up with layers upon layers of other people's "you should's," "you must's," and "you really ought to's."

Paying the Price for Fitting In

When you think about the cultural consciousness in the United States, it's not surprising that many of us have worked so hard to belong—it is part of the American psyche to be politically and socially correct, to know what's in, what's out, what's acceptable, what is taboo. **We are brought up in this country to fit in rather than find out who we are.** And those who are different and do not fit in are made to suffer and feel like failures.

When I was twelve years old, I was not cute and blond like the popular girls. I did not wear the right clothes, because I could not afford them. I was the only kid I knew whose parents were divorced. I had the ugliest pair of white glasses in the world. I did not fit in.

Once a month after school, I went to a dance called a Cotillion, sponsored by a local club. There in a large country club ballroom, instructors would teach all of us how to do the foxtrot or the cha-cha, and then they would line all the boys up on one side of the room, and all the girls on the other. The idea was that each boy would approach a girl and ask her to dance.

Each month, the same thing would happen: I would watch as, one by one, each girl would be chosen, until I was the only one left. And then, a very overweight boy named Martin, whose face was literally covered with freckles and whose hands were coated with sweat, would stumble across the empty floor and ask me to be his partner while the whole room watched and snickered. And as the music began, and Martin grabbed my unwilling hand, I would curse myself for being so different and so unacceptable, and wonder if I'd ever know what it was like to fit in.

I soon found out. By the time I was in junior high school, and continuing into senior high, I'd become one of the most popular girls in our class. I finally felt accepted. But like anyone desperate for approval, I was petrified of losing my status by making a social mistake. And so I only befriended the other popular kids, regardless of what kind of people they were, or how uninteresting they might have been, and ignored the kids I really wanted to get to know—the artists, the musicians, or the quiet, unassuming young men and women in my honors classes who had great minds. I am ashamed to say that I became exactly what I had hated so much when I was the social outcast. *I didn't want to be friends with someone who did not fit in.*

When I look back on this time of my life, I feel tremendous regret for my behavior. **I missed out because I was so afraid of being left out.** I was so hungry to belong, to be accepted, that I was willing to lose myself in order to have a few people

I could call friends. Of course, they did not know the real me. They only knew the part of me I thought they would approve of—the rest I hid carefully away.

When we graduated, everyone wondered why I chose to attend a college in the Midwest when all of the kids in my crowd were attending the Ivy League schools on the East Coast. I myself wondered why I made the decision to head toward Wisconsin, away from everything familiar to me—that is, until I got there and found something I hadn't even realized I was looking for: FREEDOM! Suddenly, I was free from everything and everyone I had ever looked to for approval. For the first time in my life, I began to explore who Barbara really was, and that was the beginning of the first stage of my rebirth. I know now that I could never have found myself if I had stayed in Philadelphia. My desire to belong, with its roots in that awkward, unattractive little girl on the Cotillion floor carrying around so much pain, was greater than my desire to be me.

So Martin, wherever you are: *Forgive me for not seeing that you felt just as ashamed and rejected as I did, that we were kindred souls back then. I hope, like me, you've finally found your dignity, and that whoever your dancing partner is now always looks proudly up at you when you take her in your arms.*

✦

"It takes a lot of courage to release the familiar and seemingly secure, to embrace the new. But there is no real security in what is no longer meaningful. There is more security in the adventurous and exciting, for in movement there is life, and in change there is power."

—ALAN COHEN

Each time you gave up a dream, a belief, a desire, or a habit because it wouldn't be approved of, or you wouldn't fit in, or it wasn't what was expected, or it just wasn't done, or because of what the neighbors or your mother or your relatives would think, you gave away a piece of yourself. *The more pieces you gave up, the less of yourself was left.* In some cases, you might have become so buried under piles of other people's values, that when you attempt to find yourself, there is no one there. And when you don't know who you are, you cannot experience real and meaningful moments either alone or with others.

> When you compromise your dreams and your values for someone else's, you give your power away. The more you have sacrificed your authenticity, the more disempowered you will feel.

How do you begin to take your power back? You start by rediscovering your own truth, your own values, your own voice, and living it every day.

When a child is born, she leaves behind her mother's womb, and is cut free from the cord that bound her, by breath and blood, to her first home. This exodus is necessary for the infant's survival. She can no longer grow while she is still enclosed within those walls, and that which once nurtured her will soon become that which destroys her, unless she breaks free.

In this way, giving birth to yourself means leaving behind parts of yourself that no longer nourish you, and cutting your connection to all of the beliefs, values, and obligations you've taken on that were not yours to begin with. It means saying good-bye to the person others have expected you to be, and reinventing yourself as the person *you* want to be.

◆

"Nothing is at last sacred but the integrity of your own mind."
— EMERSON

On the road back to yourself, the first stop is integrity.
Living with integrity means that who you appear to be is who you really are. Your beliefs, your values, your commitments—your inner realities— are all reflected in how you live your life on the outside. The more you live as who you truly are, the more peace you will invite into your life.

Living with integrity means:

✦ Not settling for less than what you know you deserve in your relationships
✦ Asking for what you want and need from others
✦ Speaking your truth, even though it might create conflict or tension
✦ Behaving in ways that are in harmony with your personal values
✦ Making choices based on what you believe, and not what others believe

Living without integrity takes a lot of energy. It is intellectually and emotionally exhausting, because who you are on the inside and how you behave on the outside are not **congruent** with one another.

Imagine that you are standing on a river, with each of your feet in a different boat. One boat represents your values, and the other represents your behavior. You start floating down the river. As long as the two boats remain close together, you're fine. But when one starts to drift farther away from the other, it will become difficult to straddle both craft. The farther apart the two boats get, the harder it will be for you to keep a foot in each, until at one point, the two boats become too distanced from one another, and you fall into the water.

The farther your own behavior drifts from your values, the more difficult it will become for you to function happily each day, and the more internal anxiety you'll experience. You will have to stretch too far to stay psychologically and spiritually afloat. At some point, your system will just break down. This can take the form of physical illness, mental stress or collapse, and emotional turmoil.

Running an Integrity Check

Here is a simple way to begin noticing all of the places where you are out of integrity with your values, and it's something you can start practicing as soon as you put down this book:

Each hour, on the hour, check with yourself to see if anything you've done or said in the past sixty minutes was not congruent with who you are.

Replay the past hour in your mind as if you're watching a movie, and *wherever you feel an uncomfortable feeling, stop the movie and notice what was happening.* Were you pretending the sarcastic comment your husband made didn't bother you? Were you silently listening to a friend judge someone you care about, without defending that person? Were you eating something you know was unhealthy, that you promised yourself you'd stay away from?

You will be amazed at how many times a day you betray yourself by smiling when you are really hurt, holding back love when you want to reach out, agreeing to do something that does not feel right to you, or showing the parts of yourself that someone is comfortable with rather than being who you truly are.

Let's say you do this integrity exercise, and find you're averaging five incidents an hour during which you are not being 100 percent authentically who you are. Now multiply the number of hours you are awake (say, sixteen) by five and you get eighty. Take the eighty little acts you perform or communications you express each day that are not congruent with your inner self, multiply them by 365, and your total is 29,200. That means, **29,200 times each year, you betray your own values and beliefs, you do or say something that doesn't feel right inside.** And each time this happens, you create physical and emotional stress in your system.

Now, let's say you are forty-five years old. We won't count the first eight years of your life in our equation, since most children are quite authentic until they "mature" and begin editing themselves in order to get approval. So you would subtract 8 from 45, which leaves 37, and then multiply *37 years × 29,200 incidents.* That equals: **1,080,400!!!** 1,080,400 times in your life so far when you've been untrue to yourself, **1,080,400 times when you were not living on the outside as who you are on the inside.**

No one betrays us as much in our lives as we
betray ourselves.

Is it any wonder then, that by the time we reach even our late twenties, we begin feeling uneasy with ourselves, and by our thirties and forties, we are often in the midst of spiritual turmoil? And what of real moments? How can we experience them when we, *the experiencers,* are not even fully experiencing ourselves?

If you start today doing an Integrity Check each hour, you will soon notice that you are behaving much more congruently in all areas of your life. You'll catch yourself about to betray your values, and in that moment, you'll have the freedom to choose to be authentically who you truly are. By the end of just one week of Integrity Checks, you will feel more powerful and more peaceful than you have in a long while.

You will be ready to discover the real moments that have always been there, waiting to bring you joy.

✦

"The important thing is this: To be able at any moment to sacrifice what we are for what we could become."
— CHARLES DU BOIS

Right about the time I began working on *Real Moments,* I made a business trip to New York. One afternoon I found myself stuck in bumper-to-bumper traffic in the backseat of a taxi cab. The driver and I began talking, and when he found out I was an author, and that I was writing a book about living life with meaning, he lit up. "This is right up my alley!" he proclaimed. And he proceeded to tell me his story:

The Taxi Driver's Secret for Finding Happiness

"You know, I didn't always drive a cab," he explained. "I used to be in sales. I drove then too, but I was away from home most of the week. Didn't see my wife and kids much in those days. I was making good money, and going on a fast track, you know, to try and keep up with the other guys in the company. I guess I thought I'd made it. You know, my dad was a pipe fitter—came over from Poland when he was sixteen, before the war. He really never got the hang of English, but he was good with his hands. I knew he always wanted better for me, and so I felt pretty good driving around in a nice suit and closing deals.

"Well, one day about ten years ago, my youngest son got hit by a car while crossing the street. Oh, he's O.K. now, but he was really bad for a while. The thing was, my wife couldn't find me. I was out on the road, driving between some town and another, and didn't call in until the day after the accident happened. When I finally reached her, she was hysterical. She told me our son might not make it, and how could I not be there, and she couldn't live like this anymore.

"I hightailed it home from Ohio in seven hours—a record. And when I walked into that hospital room, and saw my little boy lying there with tubes stuck in him, all wrapped up in white bandages, I fell apart. My wife looked like hell, my youngest daughter wouldn't stop crying, and in that moment, I realized that things hadn't been right for a while with all of us. I was never home. That kind of says it all, doesn't it? Sure, we had nice things, and sure, my pop was proud of me, but we didn't have a life together. Jeez, what if my son had died when I was away? It could have happened, you know. Right then and there, I made a decision. I didn't care what it took, I was going to get my life back again.

"That's when I quit my job and bought the cab. A real glamorous promotion, right!! Hey, but you know what? The last ten years have been the best of my life. I got to see my kids grow up, and all three of them are doing great. My wife and I got our marriage going again. Now she's my best friend, and I sure as heck wouldn't have said that ten years ago. And we saved up enough to buy a little cottage on a lake upstate. It's not much, but every Friday we drive up and spend the weekend. I'll tell you, when I'm sitting on my porch looking out at the trees and the water, I feel terrific, you know what I mean?"

I did. I had just met a truly happy man. He had lost himself, like so many of us have, and then he had given birth to himself again, finding his own way home.

I told him that I was so impressed with his story, I was going to put it in my book, and he was thrilled. "My wife won't believe this!" He laughed.

"Tell me something," I said. "If you had one piece of advice based on all you've learned about how to be happy, what would it be?"

He was quiet for a minute, and then he replied:
"To be happy, you have to say 'no' to things."

The Power of "No"

I am sure that God placed that cab driver in my path for a reason. I needed to learn the power of "no." I'd been living my life by a different aphorism:
"To be successful, you have to say 'yes' to things."
I said "yes" to all the projects that came my way, "yes" to all the opportunities to give a speech, "yes" whenever my staff asked me to put on another seminar that would help people, "yes" whenever a friend needed advice, no matter what time of night or day. My phone rang constantly, my schedule had no free sections, and listening to the driver describe his cottage on the lake, I felt like giving up everything and buying a cab myself!! He had made real moments a priority in his life, by recommitting to his own new values, and saying "no" to values that no longer served him.

> We need to find the courage to say "NO" to the things that are not serving us if we want to rediscover ourselves and live our lives with authenticity.

I can tell you from experience that this is not as easy as it sounds. Saying "no" can mean cutting ties you have had for a long time to people, places, things, and ideas. It can mean making decisions that others do not approve of. It can mean letting go of old values and identities before you've quite developed the new ones, and being in a state of emotional limbo for a while—you know you aren't who you used to be, but you aren't quite sure yet who you are becoming.
But hidden within every "no" is a "yes." When you say "no"

to doing something that does not feel right anymore, you are saying "yes" to strengthening your own integrity. When you say "no" to remaining friends with people who do not support your growth or new direction, you are saying "yes" to the new friends who will soon be arriving in your life. When you say "no" to selling out your principles and ideals in order to get ahead in business, you are saying "yes" to a new level of self-respect. When you say "no" to not being treated as you deserve to be in a relationship, you are saying "yes" to loving and protecting yourself.

As I look back on my life, it has always been saying "no" to something that has been the first step in each of my most powerful emotional and spiritual transformations.

My First Big "No"

I was a senior in high school before I learned to use the power of "no." It was 1969, and our school had a strict dress code—no pants for girls, and no blue jeans for boys. Everyone thought this was stupid—in the winter, the temperature would go down to fifteen degrees, and the girls would be trudging through two feet of snow wearing stockings and little short skirts. And the boys were allowed to wear black jeans, and green jeans, but not blue. God forbid someone should think we had a bunch of farmers attending our school. As secretary of the student council, I tried for months to talk with the principal and have the dress code changed, but he wouldn't budge. So I decided to organize a strike!

I don't recall why I chose this issue on which to take my first stand. Perhaps it was because we were in middle of the Vietnam War, and I felt helpless to do anything that would prevent my friends from being drafted. Perhaps it was because I knew I'd be leaving for college in a few months, and didn't care anymore what people thought of me. Or perhaps I was just tired of always saying "yes" to everything and trying so hard to get everyone to like me.

For weeks, in secret, I planned our tactics. On one particular Friday morning, we would all show up wearing pants or jeans. I figured if enough kids did it, they couldn't suspend us all. The word spread through the grapevine, and finally Friday arrived. I could hardly wait to get to school to witness the uproar we would cause. So you can imagine how devastated I was to discover that *most of the students chickened out at the last minute and wore their regular clothing. Only about one hundred of us had dared to defy the dress code.*

Within fifteen minutes after the first bell rang, the principal called a special assembly. The whole school, 1,800 of us, gathered together in the auditorium. "Apparently some of you do not know the meaning of the word 'rule,'" he began in his droning voice. "It has come to my attention that a radical group of students attempted to lead a strike this morning in protest over our dress code. Naturally, this infringement of school policy will not be tolerated. Those students will be asked to return home and come back to school when they are properly attired. The rest of us will resume class as usual. If anyone has any information about the instigators of this plot, please see me or the vice-principal."

When I remember this now, I laugh at how ridiculous the situation was—our principal trying to exert some last measures of control over us before we went off to college, the students being too afraid to defy him, and me feeling abandoned by everyone who had promised to lend their support. But at the time, I wasn't laughing. I was angry—angry at those in authority for not respecting my values, and angry with my friends for not being more courageous.

None of us ever got suspended for our strike. But I paid the price for organizing it. At our graduation ceremony several months later, I didn't receive any of the awards and scholarships I'd been told by my teachers I would get. All of them were given to another girl who never questioned school policy or took a stand on anything. I remember sitting on the stage in my cap and gown with the other three elected student council members, and watching people whisper to one another as this girl's name and not mine was called over and over again. I could just imagine the parents using this as a lesson for their children: *"See what happens when you go against the rules?"*

I can't say I was not hurt and disappointed that I didn't receive the honors I'd worked so hard for. However, what I did get was far more important: **I found my voice, and a piece of myself that had been buried for years under my hunger for acceptance. By speaking out for what I believed was right, I had taken an important first step in giving birth to myself.**

In the end, the power of "no" triumphed after all. A year after I graduated, the dress code was finally changed so the students could wear what they wanted to school. But that's not the end of the story. Four years ago, twenty-one years after I graduated, I received a letter from my high school announcing that they wanted to elect me to the Hall of Fame, along with other famous graduates like baseball great Reggie Jackson, since, and I quote, **"you have become someone we can all be proud of."** I called my mother and laughed for ten minutes on the phone!! I haven't made it back there yet to attend the ceremony or receive my award in front of the present student body, but believe me, when I do, I will make sure to say what I never got a chance to say twenty-five years ago in that same auditorium—*that education would serve us better by teaching us to give birth to ourselves as individuals, rather than trying to get us to conform to other people's ideas of who and what we should be.*

✦

As we journey toward wholeness, rediscovering our own values and standing by them is one of the most significant ways we can live authentically and experience more real moments. Here is one of my favorite stories about integrity. I don't recall where I first heard it, but I pass it on every chance I get:

Once there was a young Jewish boy who lived in a small town located in what was then the Russian Empire around the turn of the century. This was a time when there was great persecution of the small population of Jews in each village by the Cossacks, the Czar's soldiers. Every day during market hours, as the townspeople gathered in the main square to do their business, the Cossacks would ride into town on their powerful horses, scatter the goods and wares of the Jews, read the latest edict from the Czar limiting the Jews' freedom, and then ride off.

Now, this young boy was exceedingly fond of his grandfather, who happened to be the old Rabbi of the village. All the Jews in town agreed that their Rabbi was as wise as Abraham or Moses. Every day, the young boy would walk with his grandfather from their modest home to the center of the city. The Cossacks would come riding in, dust flying, and the soldier in charge would read the daily edict: "From today on, no Jews can buy more than five potatoes at a time," or "The Czar has ruled that all Jews must sell their best cows to the state at once."

And each day, the same thing would happen: The old Rabbi would listen along with everyone else to the edicts, and then he would raise his walking stick, shake it in the air at the Cossacks, and in a loud voice proclaim: "I protest!! I protest!!" And then one of the Cossacks would ride into the crowd, and strike the Rabbi with his riding crop yelling, "Silence, you old fool!" before riding off. The Rabbi would fall to the ground, his followers would rush to pick him up and brush the dirt from his coat, and his grandson would help him back to their house.

Day after day, month after month, the young boy watched in horror as this scene repeated itself. Finally, he could hold his tongue no more, and one day, as he escorted his bruised grandfather from the town square, the boy got up the courage to address him. "Beloved Rebbe," the boy asked in a trembling voice. "Why do you keep speaking out against the Czar each day, when you know the soldiers will just beat you? Why don't you just keep quiet?"

The Rabbi smiled kindly at his grandson and answered:

"Because by not speaking against what I know is wrong, I would become one of them. . . ."

Speak your truth—it will always lead you back home to yourself.

Making the Passage to Wholeness

Turning away from who you have been should always be done with love. After all, the birth process begins nine months earlier with an act of love. So too must your passage to wholeness begin not as a negation of your past, but an affirmation of your future. *It's not a question of determining what is good or bad in your life, but rather, what is serving you and what is holding you back.* Just because you choose a new path does not mean the old path was a bad one. Just because you take a new direction does not mean the old way was the wrong way. Just because you take on new values does not mean the old values were corrupt. **We must learn to say no without having to make what we are leaving behind wrong, or make ourselves wrong for having not left sooner.**

Leaving without judgment is especially difficult to do

when, in order to grow, you must say no to people or activities for which you feel a lot of love. Sometimes the love is so strong, you become afraid that you cannot leave if you still feel it, *so you try to kill the love in order to get the courage to break away.* I see many people do this in relationships—they know it's time to go on, but it hurts too much to do it while they still feel so much emotion. So they talk themselves into hating their partner, or in the case of work, hating their job. Then, leaving is easier, because they don't feel the pain of loss. But in the end, they robbed themselves of the love they nurtured for so long.

Nothing has to be wrong with what you've been doing for you to make changes in your life. It can just be the right time.

Saying Good-bye Over the Airwaves

One of the hardest things I've ever had to was quit my job as a radio talk show host. For two years, I had a daily show in Los Angeles. Each day, I'd try to help callers deal with the problems they'd present to me, and the program became a huge success. I had a very special relationship with my listeners—I felt protective of them when they were being mistreated, I cheered for them when they made breakthroughs, I cried with them when they experienced tragedy. They were my family, and I was theirs.

One night, I had a dream that the radio station changed its format to all news, and fired all of the talk show hosts. In the dream, I told my husband what was happening, and said, "This is great, because now I don't have to quit, and no one will be angry with me for leaving." The next morning when I woke up and remembered the dream, I knew immediately that it was time for me to let go of the show.

My dream had revealed that it was my fear of disappointing

my audience that was holding me there, along with the fact that I loved what I did so much, and couldn't imagine letting go of something I'd worked that hard to achieve. Leaving would have been easy if I hated my job. *But I knew that although staying on the air would continue to serve others, it would not serve me.* I longed for the time to write more, travel more, and challenge myself in new ways, and the job was not structured so that I could do that.

When I said good-bye during my last show, I cried and my audience cried with me. I received thousands of letters pleading with me to return. Some people even picketed the station, demanding that they do whatever it took to get me back. My office even received a few angry phone calls, accusing me of abandoning my loyal following. I watched all of this go on, knowing in my heart that I'd made the right choice, because although everyone else felt I belonged there, I knew I didn't anymore.

This was not the first or the last time in my life that following the voices which call me down my road angered people who wanted me to stay right where I was—*not because it would be good for me, but because it would be good for them.* And so I have gotten used to the labor pains that often accompany each new life I birth myself into; the tearing away that is often necessary; the forces tugging on me to stay; the temptation to give in to the voices that call: *"We won't love you if you go."* However, each time I follow my heart, I emerge from my new metamorphosis with more wholeness and more freedom than I ever imagined before. And it is these rebirths that have given me some of my most precious real moments.

✦

"The only life worth living is the adventurous life. Of such a life, the dominant characteristic is that it is unafraid. It is unafraid of what other people think . . . It does not adapt either its pace or its objectives to the pace and objectives of its neighbors. It thinks its own thoughts, reads its own books, it develops its own hopes, and it is governed by its own conscience.The herd may graze where it pleases or stampede where it pleases, but he who lives the adventurous life will remain unafraid when he finds himself alone."

— RAYMOND B. FOSDICK

I hope that reading this chapter has made you restless— restless to examine your life and discover where you are not living in integrity with your own values, restless to make some of the changes and take some of the risks you've been avoiding, restless to begin searching for the lost pieces of yourself, restless to begin dreaming again, restless for more real, authentic moments.

You are free to do this, you know. **You** *can* reinvent your life. There is no waiting period. You can begin now, right after you put this book down.

Will you feel better if I tell you that reinventing your life doesn't necessarily mean that you have to quit your job, or get a divorce, or sell everything and move to the country? *It may mean that you do the same things differently.* It may mean you take a different road to work, or that you feed your family when *you* want to, and not at 5:30 because that's when your mother always fed you. *Dozens of opportunities will come your way today, or perhaps tomorrow, to make a different choice*—to give one of your lost selves a voice, or to reveal a part of you no one has seen before, to wear or do or say something that you would have said just wasn't like you.

Who Are You?

Here are some of the questions to ask yourself as your re-birth begins. They are designed to be more like keys that will open doors to hidden places, rather than simple questions with precise responses. Think about each one carefully. Plant them deep inside of you, as you would plant a seed deep into the earth. And then be patient. Don't be in a hurry for the answer to grow.

These are good questions to talk about with people you love. They are also good to write about. As you change and rediscover more of who you really are, the answers will change. Know that just by asking these questions, your journey back to yourself and to more real moments has begun.

Who Am I?

1. In which areas have I inherited behaviors and attitudes similar to those of my family members, that are keeping me from being authentically my own person? (Communication, expressing love and affection, health habits, work ethic, political and spiritual beliefs, etc.)

2. How did my family treat (or judge) people who were different from us? How do I treat people who are different from me? Am I comfortable with being different?

3. Which of my own dreams or beliefs have I sacrificed, diminished, or put aside in order to fulfill the expectations of others?

4. What parts of myself, both in the past and the present, have I hidden from others for fear they would disapprove of me? What parts do I bury even from myself?

5. In what ways have I tried to fit in that have resulted in my compromising my values or editing myself, both now and in the past?

6. What things have I done in my life in the past that I felt I should do, even though I did not fully want to do them?

7. What things am I doing now in my life that I feel I should do, even though I do not fully want to do them?

8. What habits and traditions do I still practice that are more a reflection of other people's values rather than my own?

9. What are *my* values and beliefs? If I lived them 100 percent, how would that look in my life? How would the people close to me react?

10. Am I living where and how I want to live, or where and how someone else wants me to live? What would I have to change to have my lifestyle congruous with my desires?

11. What must I do in order to unearth the buried parts of me and bring them back to life?

12. What do I need to let go of to finally grow up?

13. Am I happy? What would make me happy?

14. What do I need to do in my life to be free?

✦

"When you die and go to Heaven, our Maker is not going to ask, 'Why didn't you discover the cure for such and such? Why didn't you become the Messiah?' The only question we will be asked in that precious moment is 'Why didn't you become you?' "
—ATTRIBUTED TO ELIE WIESEL,
author and Holocaust survivor,
paraphrasing an old Yiddish story

You are one of a kind. There has never been, and never again will be a human being like you. There is nothing ordi-

nary about you. **If you feel ordinary, it is because you have
chosen to hide the extraordinary parts of yourself from the
world.** Maybe you have even forgotten that they are there,
because it's been so long since you've last seen them.

But listen . . . they are calling to you . . . voices from within
yourself . . . crying out to be recognized, to be reunited with
one another. *"Set us free,"* they whisper, *"and we will show you
the way back to wholeness."*

You have heard the call, you have felt the movement, so
you understand that the time for your rebirth has come. Now
your labor begins:

Empty yourself of everything you
no longer need.
Make space for your emerging spirit.
Then just let go and enjoy the ride.
Remember: You already *know* how to do this.
That's how you got here in the first place. . . .

· 5 ·

REAL MOMENTS
AND WORK

"Your work is to discover your work, and then, with all your heart, to give yourself to it."

— BUDDHA

Real moments aren't just for weekends. They aren't meant to be saved for a special occasion, like a favorite article of clothing you only wear on Saturday nights, or holidays. They shouldn't be limited to walks on the beach, early morning bike rides, or cozy cuddles with your beloved. They need to be woven through the entire landscape of your life. And that includes your work.

You spend at least one half of your waking life at work, whether work means a job outside your home, such as a salesperson, or a job inside your home, such as a mother. That is a lot of time to spend doing something unless it makes you happy. This explains why so many of us return from work at the end of the day, or finish our household duties, and look like we've been run over by a truck. **It's exhausting to do something you are not fully enjoying, especially when you know you will have to do it all over again the next day.**

The spirit feeds on joy, love, and celebration. . . .

W ork without real moments dries up your
spirit, and leaves it hungry.

You know you have a hungry spirit when you sit in front
of the television at the end of the day, clicking from one channel to another, or when you open your refrigerator and stare
blankly at what's on the shelves, or when you go directly from
work to the bar down the street to have a drink and "unwind."
What you are looking for will not be found on any TV program, or in any food box or carton, or at the bottom of a glass
of beer. *Your spirit is hungry to know that the hours of this
precious day you just spent working were not spent in vain, that
they counted for something, that they had some purpose and
meaning.*

It is hard to come home and share love with your wife
when your spirit is hungry. It's hard to embrace your husband
with passion when your spirit is hungry. It's hard to sleep
deeply and dream peacefully when your spirit is hungry.

You would not neglect to feed your body during the day.
So, too, you must not neglect to nourish your spirit.

Finding Your True Vocation

Sometimes, we feel it is difficult to have real moments filled
with meaning during the day because of the kind of job we
do. "I'm a cashier at a supermarket," you think to yourself.
"How can my job feed my spirit?" The answer is: *Doing your
job cannot bring you real moments, but doing your Work can.*

A ll of us are here on this Earth with Work to
do, but your Work has nothing to do
with your job.

✦ Your **job** is what you do to survive physically, and to support yourself and your family. It is the profession you choose, the skills you develop.

It is being a painter, a plumber, a computer programmer, an archeologist.

✦ Your **Work** is what you do to survive emotionally, and to support your spirit. It is the lessons you are here to learn, the wisdom you are here to gain. It is the map for your personal Earth adventure.

Your Work Is Your Purpose.

It is learning to treat others with compassion, learning to love yourself even with your imperfections, learning forgiveness, learning courage, learning trust, learning love.

✦

"You need not wait until you are older, wiser, and mature enough to accept a wonderful job from God."

— MARCELLA DANIELS

Another word for Work is **vocation**. Most people think "vocation" refers to the job you have or the career you've chosen. But the word vocation is derived from the Latin *vocatio,* which means *call* or *summons.* So your "vocation" literally means **your calling.**

Each of us has a calling, something unique to contribute to the world, something valuable to share with the people we love and live with. **Your calling is your job from God**, Job with a capital "J"! What kind of jobs does God give us as humans?

✦ To be kind to one another
✦ To take care of the Earth
✦ To enjoy God's marvelous creation as fully as possible

- ✦ To learn everything we can while we are here about being good human beings
- ✦ To love and accept ourselves and others as much as God loves us
- ✦ To remember who we really are

You do not need to prepare for these jobs, or even qualify for them. **The fact that you are here and have a physical existence means you obviously got the job!** And as for learning how to do your Work well, that's what on-the-job training is all about.

When you don't know your Purpose, or your true Vocation, you might resent your everyday job, or think you have the wrong one, because you'll expect it to fulfill your spirit, and it cannot. A job is a job. Of course, some are more suited to you than others—it's up to you to find the most enjoyable job you can. But just because you have what you consider to be an "ordinary," "boring," or "unglamorous" job, doesn't mean you cannot do the Work you are here to do. You don't have to be a minister, or a teacher, or a writer to live your purpose.

Remember my friend the cab driver? His job was to drive a taxi. His Work, his calling, was to share love with his family and all those he came into contact with, and to remember, in this life, what was truly important. From what I saw when I met him, he was very successful at both. And it was doing his real Work *while* he was on his job, as he did when he reached out so honestly to me, that gave his job meaning.

When you know what your true Work is, you can do it anytime—when you are building a house, or selling shoes, when you are cooking dinner for your family, or helping your child with her homework. And you can do it anywhere—in a store, over the phone, on a street corner . . . even in a taxi.

✦

"How many cares one loses when one decides not to be *something*, but to be *someone*."

— COCO CHANEL

Each of us has a Calling, not just the teachers and preachers of the world. I can't tell you what your Calling or your true Work is. That is for you to discover. In fact, **that's the first stage of your Work—for you to figure out your Purpose, your Calling, your gift.** But I'll give you a hint about how to begin: *Look at what is unique about you, those characteristics or abilities that distinguish you from other people, and there you will find your Vocation.*

Maybe your uniqueness lies in your ability to express yourself well with words, or to have a calming effect on others, or to make people laugh, or to understand and simplify complex situations. Maybe your gift is your voice, your strong hands, your eye for beauty, your talent for seeing the best in people. And if you aren't sure what your gift is, ask the people who know you.

Sometimes other people see our gift and Purpose before we do. Where else should you look to find your calling?

Look at what you love to do.
Look at what brings you joy.
Look at what gives you peace.
There is your calling, waiting for you to
embrace it.

Nothing in our Universe was designed without a purpose. An eagle's wing was shaped so that he could fly. A rose was given color so it would attract the honeybee. Our bodies need to rest for several hours a day, and it just so happens that the

Earth turns away from the Sun, our source of light and heat, for that same amount of time, and when we are rejuvenated, the Earth has turned back toward the Sun again. From the movement of the planets, to the movement of blood through our veins, every detail of our physical existence reflects a Higher Order.

You are a part of Creation. You are part of that Order. There is a reason for your being who and what you are. There is purpose in everything about you. *You have been given your particular and unique gifts and abilities so that you could do your particular and unique Work. It is not an accident.*

You have exactly what you need to fulfill your
Purpose here. Your wings are shaped perfectly.

✦

Why do so many of us ignore our Calling, and refuse to take up our true Vocation? *Because we make the mistake of thinking that we have to earn money doing something for it to be worth our time and energy.* It's as if we think that being paid for what we contribute is a cosmic sign that what we contribute has worth.

Receiving money for what you do is not a
validation that you are living your Purpose and
doing your real Work — receiving joy
and contentment is.

I have a friend who works as a manager in a large corporation. His job consists mostly of paperwork, meetings, and more paperwork. It pays well, but he doesn't find it fulfilling. What does satisfy him, however, is what he's always called his "outside interest" — working with underprivileged children. For ten years he has volunteered as a Big Brother to many young boys, taught basketball on weekends to kids from the inner city, and once a year he helps raise money used to sponsor poor children for a week at camp.

We spoke on the phone recently, and he told me he was thinking of quitting his job. "I feel like what I do at this company is useless, that I'm not contributing anything to society," he complained. "Maybe I should go back to school and become a social worker, or a teacher. I mean, I'm thirty-seven years old, and I'm not happy with my work."

"But you're already a social worker and a teacher and a basketball coach," I reminded him. "You're just not getting paid for it. Would it make that much of a difference if you were?"

My friend was stunned. He'd never thought about the fact that he really was living his Purpose, **because he wasn't being rewarded for it financially.** He thought about his job at the company as what he really did, and his Work with the kids as a hobby. But it was really the other way around—*his Work with the kids was his real profession, and his day job, which helped him earn a living, was his hobby.*

"So what you're saying is, everything I'm doing is fine," he proposed. "It's the way I look at it that needs to change."

"Right, " I agreed. "If it helps, think of your job at the company as what you do to pay the bills so that you can be free to fulfill your Calling as a guardian angel to those boys."

Like my friend, you may have a job that has little or nothing to do with your real Work, except that it gives you the financial freedom to do it. You are an executive secretary, but your real Work is organizing your church choir. You are an accountant, but your real Work is raising your children. You sell real estate, but your real Work is motivating your friends to be the best they can be.

Let people know what your real Work is. When you meet someone new, and they ask "What do you do?" tell them the truth: "I work at learning how to be good to myself and other people, and for a job, I cut hair," or "My real Work is being a mother and a wife, and to support myself, I am an investment counselor."

Real Moments happen
when you do the Work you came here to do.

If the first part of your Work is figuring out what your Work is, the second part is learning how to do your real Work every day. *The more opportunities you create to participate in your Purpose while you do your daily job, the more real moments you will experience.* Maybe you are a teacher, and at some point during your day you reach out to a child who is carrying a lot of personal pain, and let him know you understand, and that you care. Your day suddenly becomes meaningful, not because you went to work, but because you practiced your true Vocation while you were there. Or maybe you work in a large factory, and one afternoon you take ten minutes to convince your employer to hire a friend of yours who hasn't been able to find a job and is having a difficult time supporting his family. You go home that evening with a smile on your face—at your job, you found a way to do your Work. You feel complete.

If what you do for a living involves relating to people, then you will always be able to conjure up a real moment or two during every day. Anytime you transcend the usual, superficial way of connecting with others, and share from the heart, you can have a real moment.

Whenever you're sharing love,
you're living your Purpose.

Here's something that will help you experience more real moments during your regular work day: **Make a list of activi-**

ties, behaviors and attitudes you can incorporate into your job at work or at home that will help you live your Purpose. These will serve as reminders, so that whenever you are feeling in need of a real moment, you can pull out the list, choose to put one of the items into practice, and create an instant sense of purpose.

I suggest that you carry a copy of the list around with you, post another on your desk or refrigerator, and read them often. Here are a few items from my own list. Perhaps some of these will give you ideas for yours.

✦ Share a moment of love with someone
✦ Appreciate beautiful things in your environment
✦ Learn something new
✦ Look for an opportunity to make someone feel valuable
✦ Play with the dog
✦ Spend a few minutes in the garden watching the flowers grow
✦ Lie in the hammock and let the breeze rock you back and forth
✦ Stop and remember *why* you're doing what you are doing

When Your Job Is Bad for You

What you do as a job isn't as important as *how* you do it. If you do it with caring, if you do it with contentment, then it will be a good way to earn your living. Your job doesn't have to be an activity where you can fully express your real Work or Calling. *But it should not be an activity that goes against your Work.*

When you have a job where you must compromise your values, hide your true self, or

> participate in actions which are out of integrity,
> then your job is a place your spirit dies
> eight hours a day.

You cannot compartmentalize different portions of your life from one another. You can't have a job that is toxic to your well-being, and prevent it from affecting your relationship, your health, and your peace of mind. *If your job takes you that far off your Purpose, it will be difficult for you to get back on track at the end of the day, and after years of living incongruently, you may not be able to even find a sense of Purpose anymore.*

As I write this, I think of a woman I know who works in the entertainment industry in Los Angeles for a very well-known personality. Her job is flashy and high profile, and she makes a lot of money. There's just one problem—her boss treats her like dirt. He is rude, abusive, immature, and inconsiderate. Every time my friend calls me or we have lunch, the conversation revolves around the same two topics: how much she hates her job, and how frustrated she is that she can't meet any nice guys and get married.

For years I've listened to her complain about both sides of her life. Finally, last week I couldn't take it anymore. "Have you ever considered that the reason you can't find a nice guy may have something to do with your staying in an abusive relationship at work?" I asked her.

"I don't like what you're saying, but don't stop," she said with a grimace.

"Well, no matter how much you feel 'It's just a job,' what you spend eight hours a day doing, year after year, affects your self-esteem and what you expect from the rest of your life. I can't see any way you can attract a really loving relationship when the one you're in at work is so unhealthy."

"But it's such a good job . . . " she replied.

"No matter how much money it pays," I reminded her, "no job is a good job if it isn't good for you."

If your job isn't good for you, get a new one. *In the end, the price you'll pay staying in a situation where you are cut off from yourself and your own integrity will be much higher than what you will temporarily lose by leaving.*

✦

"I think most of us are torn. We have at least two people at war in our body. One person wants to retire and grow fabulous tomatoes, and the other wants to stand up on a pedestal and be worshipped and get bigger and bigger and bigger until she explodes."
— BETTE MIDLER

When you mistake your job for your Purpose by taking it too seriously, you can get really messed up. You will work too hard, and have a difficult time saying "no" to anything. And when you start believing that your job is more important than someone else's, or that you're the only one who can do it, or that the world can't survive without your incredible contribution, then it's time for you to retire and grow tomatoes—or at least take an extended vacation—in order to get back in tune with what you're really here for.

Taking your job too seriously means that you either don't know you have a Purpose other than your job, or you have temporarily forgotten what it is. You will not enjoy your job when you mistakenly think that it's your Work, because then you will make every small event that occurs in the course of a day a big deal. I'm not saying that you should do your job carelessly, or without one hundred percent excellence. You shouldn't. *Just don't lose your identity in what you're doing.*

If you sell twenty-five houses this month, or close three big deals, or beat out someone else for a contract, or manage the kids and the chores effortlessly, it does not mean you are any better or more deserving inside than if you had sold nothing, lost a contract, or had kids who were out of control. Knowing that, perhaps you can be a little more forgiving of yourself and those you work with and for, when things do not go as smoothly as you wish they would.

How I Got Lost on the Way Home

I am speaking from painful experience. For many years, I confused my job as a spiritual and emotional teacher with my Purpose, and it caused me a lot of unnecessary anxiety and unhappiness. In all fairness to myself, I understand how I could have fallen prey to this misconception: *some of us are given jobs that look suspiciously like a Calling.* Health-care professionals, teachers, priests, politicians, gurus, poets, motivational speakers—we all are tempted to believe that we are among the lucky few whose job and Calling are one and the same. None of this weekend Purpose stuff for us. We get to live our Purpose through our job. How blessed we feel to have been chosen to be so important! What would the world do without us?!!!

From the time I began teaching, I believed with all my heart, and with all sincerity, that my job and Purpose were to help as many people heal emotionally as I could, and to open them up to experiencing more love in their lives. I saw great suffering around me, and wanted to use my talents and gifts to help alleviate that suffering, and make a difference in the world.

What I didn't see was that by believing my Purpose was to help people, and having a job where I did exactly that, I set myself up for a lot of pain and spiritual torment. For instance, what if I couldn't help someone? Did that mean I wasn't good at my Calling? What if someone didn't want my help? Would that mean that *they* were off purpose? What if I didn't help enough people by the end of my life (whatever "enough" was in my mind)? Wouldn't that mean I had failed to fulfill my Purpose? Wouldn't I have failed God?

And so I became an *overzealous prophet of love*. I didn't just want people to grow, they *had* to, and if I saw them resisting, I became frustrated inside. Didn't they recognize the gift I was offering them? How could they turn away from an opportunity to find their own freedom? And if I felt the people I taught were growing too slowly, or not moving through their resistance quickly enough, I became impatient inside. What was taking them so long? Didn't they realize that the fate of the world rested on their getting enlightened? Why couldn't they go as fast as I could?

Of course, I rarely shared these emotions with anyone, but I know people felt them. Once in a while someone would tell me they were afraid no matter how hard they worked on themselves, it would never be good enough for me. When I heard this, I would be shocked. Where had they gotten this idea? I loved everyone, I rejoiced at seeing them grow. How could they say they felt judged? What I did not see and what my students did not understand, was that **because I thought my Purpose was to save the world, I took any sign that I wasn't doing that not just personally, but as a cosmic disappointment.**

Naturally, when the world needs saving, one can't take time off, so I became a workaholic. How could I take long vacations when there were people in pain? How could I cancel a seminar when it might mean a couple would end up getting divorced because I hadn't been there to save them? After all, this was what I came here for, to help, not to sit around enjoying myself while other people suffered. And so I worked and I worked, and because I got such approval and gratitude for everything I was doing, I took this as a sign to keep on working.

In the beginning, I was so intense about my mission that I

didn't even enjoy the work I did. I was too uptight to have a good time. This should have been a sign that something was wrong, but I didn't know enough back then to interpret it correctly. "The reason I'm not happy," I concluded, "is that I haven't helped enough people yet."

Looking back, I guess you could say that I sometimes acted like a *cranky guru.* I'd get annoyed at one of my assistants if they didn't put the chalkboard on the stage at the right time. I'd be critical of an employee for missing the deadline for an ad. I'd be upset with someone I was helping for not taking my advice. When I look back on this period now, I cringe with remorse, even though I understand the source of my unpleasant behavior—*I couldn't figure out why, when I was doing such serious important work as saving the world, other people weren't taking it as seriously.*

Fortunately, I mellowed tremendously after the first seven years of this phase of my career, learning to be gentle and loving as I shared my message, and teaching from a place of compassion. But inside, the turmoil continued, and as I wrote in my first chapter, despite the success and good fortune I was experiencing, I still was not happy. That's when I knew it was time for me to become a student again, and to find some new teachers of my own who I hoped could help me understand why living my Purpose was not fulfilling me.

Up Against the Wall

I never expected to have an awakening that would so completely change my life while hanging from a fifty-foot wall by a rope, but I did. Here's the story of how it happened:

My husband, Jeffrey, is a chiropractor. Several years ago, he began talking about a well-known chiropractic lecturer and motivator he'd recently met. His name is Dr. Guy Riekeman, and he travels around the world teaching doctors about how to find and live their Purpose. "You have to meet this man," Jeffrey kept encouraging me, "and I really want to do his ropes course with you."

A ropes course is a series of physical challenges such as standing on top of a telephone pole and jumping off, walking on wires fifty feet off the ground, or climbing a sheer wall with only tiny crevices in which to place your hands and feet. Safety ropes are used, such as those used by mountain climbers. The purpose of a ropes course is not to master the physical feats, but to face the psychological and spiritual "walls" we all carry around with us, and to experience breakthroughs by triumphing over those limitations.

I've always had a lot of emotional courage in my life, but not much physical courage. So I wasn't thrilled with the idea of leaping off a telephone pole and trusting that the people on the ground would pull my rope taut in time. But it scared me so much to think about it that I knew I had to go. Besides, I was hungry for some new breakthroughs.

✦

It was snowing that day in the Colorado mountains as we began our ropes course, led by Guy. As I put on my safety helmet and my special mountaineering vest with hooks and cables running through it, I was scared to death. I didn't think I'd even be able to climb halfway up a telephone pole, let alone leap off it. So I can't describe how proud of myself I was when, several hours later, I jumped off the pole into midair, or walked a few steps on thin wires high above the ground while holding hands with Jeffrey. And as the day progressed, and I was able to accomplish each challenging exercise, I thought I was doing great—that is until we got to The Wall.

Imagine a fifty-foot wall rising from the ground, totally flat except for a few dozen tiny cement protrusions scattered randomly over the surface. Three people are connected together with about six feet of rope separating them. The idea is for all of them to get to the top of The Wall, and obviously, either they all make it or none do, because they're tied together. I remember standing in the freezing cold, my parka pulled tight, and watching the first team strain to climb up The Wall, finally making it to the platform on the top. It looked hard, harder than anything we'd done all day.

Guy tied me and my two teammates together, me in the middle, and the climb began. I stretched my leg up in front of me, and barely reached the first tiny peg. With all my strength, I grabbed on to another peg also almost out of reach, and pulled myself up the first few feet. Already, I was out of breath—we were 10,000 feet above sea level, and the air was thin and icy. Out of the corner of my eye, I noticed both of my teammates were much higher up than me, as high as they could go while they were still attached. For the next fifteen minutes I worked harder than I ever had in my life at anything to make it up about fifteen feet.

But now I was in trouble. My body was trembling uncontrollably. My legs were cramping. My hands were so cold that I could not feel them anymore. I still had thirty-five feet to go, and my teammates had been patiently waiting for me to catch up. I looked around desperately for pegs to grab, but they all seemed too far away. I would summon all my energy, and lunge at one of them, only to fall off the pegs and dangle in the air by the safety ropes my team on the ground were holding tight.

The group had been coaching and cheering me along throughout, and now they intensified their efforts. "Come on, Barbara," they shouted from below me, "You can do it. Don't stop now. Just try going up one more peg." The more they encouraged me, the worse I felt. I made a few more pathetic tries at pushing my body up higher on the sheer wall, and each time, I'd fall back as the crowd below gasped.

I began to cry. "I can't go any farther," I moaned. "I don't have the strength. I'm so sorry. I know I'm ruining it for my partners." This only seemed to fuel my supporters, who intensified their cheering, which only made me cry harder, hot angry tears. *Why couldn't they see that I was finished? Why didn't they understand that I just couldn't do it?*

Then I heard Jeffrey's voice. "I know you can do it, baby," he shouted. "Don't give up. Don't give in to your fear! Just dig deeper and find your strength, and try to go a little higher. "

"I can't," I shrieked back in a choked voice. "I want to come down."

"Yes you can," he insisted, the crowd agreeing with him. "You can do it!"

I began to sob hysterically, because I knew Jeffrey was wrong—**I now realized, probably for the first time in my life, that no matter how hard I tried, how much I pushed myself, how intensely I wanted it, I could go no farther. I** couldn't make it. I couldn't even move one muscle anymore. I was completely paralyzed. I clung to The Wall, overcome with a sense of failure that I had never known before. *I had let my partners down, and held them back from reaching their goal. I had let Jeffrey down. Most of all, I had let myself down.*

How I Learned to Stop Pushing People and Start Loving Them

It seemed like an eternity that I hung there on that lonely mountaintop, my lungs screaming with pain, my body cramped and frozen, my heart breaking. Finally, I heard Guy's voice say "I think she's at her limit. Let's get her down."

I hardly remember letting go of The Wall, and being lowered down to the ground in my harness. But when I felt the earth once again beneath my feet, I collapsed onto the snow, weeping, and felt Jeffrey reaching for me, and then cradling me in his arms.

"I'm here, sweetheart," he whispered. "I won't leave you."

"*I'm sorry. I'm so sorry. I just couldn't do it. Please forgive me. I'm so sorry.*" That's all I could say through my tears, over and over again.

"Shhhhhhh," he comforted me. "You did great. I'm so proud of you for even trying. I saw how much you pushed yourself, honey. You have nothing to apologize for."

"I feel so terrible," I sobbed. "I didn't want to disappoint you. I wanted so badly to make you proud of me. But I just couldn't do it. I just couldn't go any farther. *I just couldn't keep up with the others.*"

Jeffrey looked at me with tenderness and compassion, and softly said: "**Barbara, that's how everyone else in your life always feels around you.**"

When I heard his words, it was as if a veil lifted from my eyes. In that moment, I got the truth about myself as a teacher and as a person, realized how I'd been misunderstanding my Purpose. Jeffrey was right. That was how everyone felt around me—*like no matter how fast they went, I could go faster; like no matter how hard they tried, I would push them to try harder; like they were always slowing me down, and would never be able to keep up.*

On The Wall that afternoon had been the hearts and souls of all my students, my lovers, my friends, who, so many times, in so many ways, had cried out to me as I had to my team that day, "I just can't go any farther. I can't go any faster." And the voices that came from below, urging me on with the best of intentions even as they ignored my pain represented my own voice, as I had been using it to motivate, to push, to implore the people I served to go farther. And as I lay in a cold bundle on the ground, I saw the truth:

. . . *That everyone in my life had always been growing as*

*fast as they could, and that what they had needed from me all
along was exactly what I'd needed that day from my team and
from Jeffrey—not judgment, not disappointment, but love.*

*. . . I needed Jeffrey to love me, even though I couldn't climb
to the top of The Wall.*

. . . I needed to know that wherever I got to was enough.

*. . . I needed to know that it wasn't reaching the destination
that made my climb a success, but just the act of climbing
itself.*

I learned more about being a teacher that day, clinging to
The Wall, than I had during all my years of giving seminars. I
learned that a teacher respects The Wall, and the process every climber goes through. A teacher knows when to say "keep
climbing," and when to say "come down." *And a teacher knows
that, ultimately, there is no up or down, high or low, no better
or worse—there's just The Wall and what the climb teaches you.*

I will always be eternally grateful to Guy Riekeman for fa-
cilitating such a crucial breakthrough in my spiritual growth,
and to Jeffrey for so wisely and lovingly telling me the truth
in a moment when I was finally ready to hear it.

Saving the World as a Hobby

Facing my own wall of misunderstanding changed me pro-
foundly. After my experience in Colorado, I taught from a
level of unconditional love and compassion I had not pre-
viously reached before. And I was happier than I'd ever been
in my life. But I knew my rebirth was not complete. I still felt
compelled to work seven days a week and overschedule myself, because I still felt responsible for "saving the world."

And then, I began to write this book. I knew when I chose
the book's topic that writing it would force me to examine
myself in a way that only writing does. *For me, working on a
book is like a twelve-month seminar.* Every day, every night,
every waking moment for a year is spent thinking about, talk-

ing about and writing about a topic—in this case, real moments and the search for meaning.

So each day as I wrote this for you, I'd read the pages and think about myself. **Was I happy? Was I hiding from real moments? What was my Purpose?**

Slowly, powerfully, I began to understand. As long as I, with my intensely passionate personality, believed that my Purpose, or even my job, was to do my part to save the world, I could not relax in my life, or focus on my own happiness. After all, I take whatever job I do very seriously. But now I saw that my job and my purpose were two different things:

My job was to be a teacher.

And my Purpose, my true Work, was to learn to celebrate my existence here on Earth, to love myself and others fully, and to be happy.

As for saving the world, as a friend of mine suggested, I could do it *"as a hobby!"* But my first responsibility was to save myself, and to experience as many real moments as possible.

This new understanding gave me the gift of freedom. I could do my job, which is teaching, *when* I was actually teaching, not twenty-four hours a day. *My acts of contribution to others, my moments of vision for our planet, could now become acts of love, and moments of joy, rather than full-time burdens, and cosmic obligations.* **I had finally given myself permission to be happy, no strings attached.**

✦

I am aware that most people do not live their lives with the same emotional velocity as I do. *I am also very certain that there is a purpose in my life having been as dramatic and intense as it's been, and therefore, a purpose in the sharing of my story.* Teachers often use metaphor to convey their message, and in many ways my life has been structured as a living metaphor to assist me in guiding others on their journey toward love and wholeness.

You may not feel the same proportion of spiritual responsibilities as I've felt in my life, but you have your own battles which interfere with your happiness that are just as significant—battles between the obligations you've taken on to your company, your family, or whatever is important to you, and your own need for time, for joy, for peace. And although you may never have been stuck on a fifty-foot wall in the mountains, unable to go up and afraid to come down, I know you've faced your own walls of fear and disillusionment. Perhaps you are even facing one right now.

May these stories comfort you in your search for meaning. May they remind you that you are not alone. May they give you the courage to reexamine your job, to discover your real Work, and to infuse them both with real moments. You may realize that you want to sell your business and move to the country, or find a healthier company to work for, or go back to school to become a veterinarian. *Or it may be that the adjustments you need to make in order to be happier are, as they were for me, adjustments in your thinking rather than in your doing.*

✦

In the end, your Work is about creating real moments by choosing to do the simple things each day:

Greet the Sun.
Breathe deeply.
Marvel at the wonder of your body.
Make someone smile.
Scratch your dog's tummy.
See the soul behind someone's eyes.
Appreciate an everyday miracle.
Thank the land for your food.
Wave to a bird.
Tell someone you love them.
Say good night to God . . .

· 6 ·

REAL MOMENTS
IN DIFFICULT TIMES

"Sometimes we turn to God
when our foundations are shaking
only to find out that it is God
who is shaking them. . . ."
— ANONYMOUS

There are moments in your life that are so sweet, living on the earth seems like a blessing and a privilege—when you first set eyes on your newborn child; when you're lying in your lover's arms early in the morning listening to the rain fall against the window; on that first day when you notice Spring's arrival, and the air is filled with promise and anything seems possible. And there are times in your life when it all seems to make sense, when things happen the way you planned them, when it is easy to believe in God and a magnificent Intelligence, for who or what else could have created a world so abundant in miracles.

Then, there are the difficult times—times when you've lost something you worked hard for, or someone you loved, times when your faith in goodness is tested, times when you just want the pain to go away. And nothing makes sense, and none of it seems worth it, and it's hard to believe in anything.

If you are old enough to read this, you have already gone through many difficult times in your life. Perhaps you're even going through one right now. One thing is for sure: *As long as we are alive, we will move in and out of crisis and adversity, and our joys will live alongside of our sorrows.*

Life on our earth is about change. In fact, you are alive because you are changing continually, and change always contains death and rebirth. At this very moment, there are cells dying and being reborn in every organ and muscle of your body. When your physical body stops changing and regenerating itself, it ceases to exist—that's called Death.

This cycle of destruction before creation is omnipresent in our physical universe. The orange blossom on a tree has to die before the fruit can grow. The seed must die before a plant can emerge as wheat must die in the making of bread. As the late Joseph Campbell emphasized so insightfully, *"You can't make an omelet without breaking eggs."*

> What went before must change form in order
> to rebirth itself, and in the process, the old form
> needs to be discarded.

It's easy to be philosophical and even accepting of change when you're talking about fruit and wheat, but it's a lot more challenging when you're talking about your own life. *As human beings, we cherish the familiar.* We cling to our routines, our daily rituals, our favorite chair, our parking spot, our side of the bed, in an attempt to give ourselves some sense of certainty and control over what we secretly know is a totally unpredictable universe. *And so we are frightened of change*—it **robs us of the safety we are accustomed to and plunges us into emotional free-fall.**

This is our dilemma—for as sure as the earth continues to turn, change will come. And it will always come in the form of loss—when we lose our youth, our hair, our figures, when we lose our jobs, our dreams, or our energy to make them come true. The loss will come when our children grow up and we lose their innocent, unconditional love, when we grow apart from those we were once close with, when death takes our grandparents and then our parents from us, and suddenly we are the elders in the family. The loss will come when our friends or our beloved passes from the world, and we are agonizingly alone. The loss will come as we age and are no longer the vital, molten core of our society, but the softer, quieter edges. The loss will come, ultimately, as we slip out of the harbor of our body and sail back into the realm of spirit.

Life is a series of painful good-byes, and good-byes are never easy. But on the other side of good-bye is hello; on the other side of releasing the old is embracing the new.

> The journey in between what you once were
> and who you are now becoming is where the
> dance of life really takes place.

In this way, difficult times are usually those times when the greatest amount of change is occurring. They may not be enjoyable times, and they certainly aren't comfortable times, but they are potent with opportunities for great awakening. And they are ripe for real moments.

✦

Difficult times make real moments more available to you because they open doors to your inner world that you may normally keep locked. When you are faced with crisis or trauma, the pain is so great that your usual filters which numb you to your emotions don't work. It is impossible to be distracted from what's going on inside of you. *You are forced to feel everything. And it's in fully feeling whatever is happening to you right then that you experience a real moment.*

Think back to a painful time in your life. Perhaps it was when you were going through a divorce, or when you were ill, or when someone in your family was in trouble. If you are like most people, you will be able to reflect back on that difficult period and say: "As much as it hurt, that *divorce, illness, tragedy, accident, etc.* was one of the best things that ever happened to me." From where you stand now, you can clearly see the gift that was hidden inside the problem. You learned things you needed to learn.

Crisis forces you to pay attention, to your life, to your relationships, and to yourself. It acts like a high-powered searchlight that focuses its beam so intensely on something, illuminating it in every detail, that you can't see anything else. And it is in those moments of powerful self-reflection and personal revelation that real moments happen.

✦

"Out of every crisis comes the chance to be reborn."
— NENA O'NEILL

From the womb of darkness, each day the dawn emerges. From the womb of adversity, you emerge with added wisdom and strength. *This is the power of difficulty—it forces you to tap into reserves of courage, hope, and love you weren't aware you possessed.*

Pain helps you to unfold yourself, to discover
the hidden treasures of spiritual wealth you did
not know existed within you.

Dan Millman, who's written several wonderful books about what he calls the "peaceful warrior," has a great saying about difficult times: *"Tragedies serve as an express elevator to Spirit."* With nowhere else to turn, we turn within, and find new connections to a source of comfort and clarity. Would we have discovered those inner realms eventually? Perhaps. But our pain and desperation accelerated the process. I've often talked to friends going through hard times who reported this same experience—that as much as they hated the awful circumstance in which they found themselves, they simultaneously felt new levels of personal power, and even peace.

> We don't develop courage by being happy every day. We develop it by surviving difficult times and challenging adversity.

Pain nourishes courage. Mary Tyler Moore, who has faced and surmounted many serious personal and physical difficulties in her own life, said it very simply: *"You can't be brave if you've only had wonderful things happen to you."*

Whenever I'm interviewed by a reporter, or speak in front of a large group, I am frequently asked the question: "What has contributed the most to your having so much knowledge about life at such a young age?" My answer is always the same: "PAINFUL EXPERIENCE!" And it's true. As I look back on the times in my life that taught me the most, they were the difficult times. By surviving them, I gained a confidence in myself I never could have achieved if I'd led a totally happy life.

It is not easy to accept difficult times as gifts rather than unjust punishments. When you are in the middle of tragedy or heartbreak, it feels like God has singled you out for misery. "I don't care if there is some cosmic lesson in this," your spirit screams from within, "I just want the pain to stop!" I don't think you'd be human if you didn't recoil from unhappiness. *But never judge yourself for how you endure your suffering—*

there is no right or wrong way to experience hardship. Disliking difficult times does not mean you have less faith, or are less enlightened. It just means you haven't completely unwrapped the gift yet . . . *What's miraculous is that, in spite of your attitude toward adversity, and regardless of how willingly or unwillingly you move through it, move through it you will—and on the other side, new strength and wisdom will be waiting.*

Whenever I am faced with difficult times, I remember something my first guru taught me in a meditation course twenty-five years ago:

"The wind blows strong and hard on the
tender young trees, not to harm them, but to
teach their roots to hold firmly to the ground."

My life has been very windy. And there have been times when I have cursed the wind for the disruption it's caused me. But now I have grown into a tall, strong tree, with powerful roots. I bless the painful moments in my life, and I thank the wind. Its relentless force has molded me into the woman I am today.

Learning to Dance with Your Pain

I once heard a saying: *"You can't stop the waves, but you can learn to surf."* Surfing means learning to ride the waves, to move in the direction the current is taking you. **And that's the best method I've discovered for dealing with pain and crisis—to move deeper into it, rather than away from it.**

You can create real moments in difficult times
by surrendering to your pain, rather than
resisting it.

I call this *learning to dance with your pain,* to find the rhythm of the challenging time you are in, and to attune yourself to it. Learning to dance with your pain means not avoiding your feelings of discomfort or fear, but choosing instead to consciously explore them. It means talking about the very thing you would rather forget. It means giving yourself the time and space to indulge in the sadness or grief.

About nine years ago, just before Christmas, the man I loved and was living with at the time walked out on me. He didn't give me any logical explanations—he just packed up and left. I suspected that he was cheating on me, which I later found out was true. But when it happened, all I knew was that he was gone, I was alone, and my heart was broken.

For several days I battled the overwhelming pain and terror I felt. I talked on the phone incessantly to anyone who would listen; I wrote him letter after letter, and then tore them up; I reread all the cards he'd ever sent me, searching for a clue as to why he'd left. Each night I would cry myself to sleep, praying that the next day would somehow be better, and each morning I would wake up, and as soon as I remembered what was happening, I'd be swallowed up by the pain all over again.

I don't know what made me decide to go away by myself for Christmas. I suddenly knew I had to get away to somewhere isolated from my friends and the television and all other distractions. I spent several days researching the right spot for a retreat. Then I heard about a tiny cabin set on some hills in Cambria, California, a little town halfway between Los Angeles and San Francisco. The owner of the cabin told me that it was beautiful but rustic—no heat, no electricity—just wood and glass looking out onto a grove of trees. "It's the perfect place for solitude," he agreed. And that's exactly what I wanted. *I needed to be alone with my pain.*

I packed up my car and drove up the coast. And for the next four days, I didn't speak to a soul. I wrote in my journal,

I meditated, I walked in the woods and along the beach during the day, I sat by candlelight surrounded by total silence at night. **I stopped resisting what was happening to me, and instead, surrendered to my pain and loss completely.**

And an amazing thing began to happen—I started to fill up with a deep, comforting sense of peace. I felt my own spirit, and experienced once again my connection to the Whole. I felt protected and soothed, as if I were being watched over in my time of trials. And as my vision cleared, I saw truths about the relationship I had not wanted to face before, and I finally let go. The intense pain began to disappear, and in its place was a dull ache, the kind you have when you've been wounded, but are now healing.

Many years have passed since that Christmas in the cabin, but I still consider those four days when I learned how to dance with my pain some of the most meaningful and precious real moments in my life. *By surrendering to my time of crisis and moving into it, rather than away from it, I rebirthed myself into a new level of clarity and serenity.* I passed through the dark night of the soul and emerged into light.

Joseph Campbell writes:

> *"The dark night of the soul comes just before revelation. When everything is lost, and all seems darkness, then comes the new life and all that is needed."*

Finding Love in the Darkness

Times of crisis draw people together. They bring out the best in our human nature. They elicit our compassion, our generosity, our innate kindness. They help us transcend our differences and celebrate our oneness. We see this every time there is a flood or an earthquake or a hurricane. *The forces of love always rally to guide us through the dark days.*

Difficult times always create opportunities for
you to experience more love in your life.

Finding love in the darkness is simple. Reach out to others
in your despair, and they will reach back. Say "I need help,"
and miraculously, help will appear. You have so many more
resources in your life than you realize—friends, acquaintances, people who love you. "I didn't know so many people
cared," you think to yourself as you receive cards or phone
calls, or offers of assistance. Sometimes it takes a tragedy or
loss for us to acknowledge how loved we truly are. This is one
of the reasons difficult times can be rich with real moments—
because they are rich with love.

◆

Last year, a friend of mine died of the AIDS virus. His name
was Jon Gould, and he was only thirty-nine years old. Jon was
a gentle, kind man in the truest sense of the word, and his life
was dedicated to service and self-discovery. When his family
and companion asked me to conduct Jon's memorial service,
I felt honored, but I was a little nervous about how it would
turn out. I wanted to do justice to Jon's beautiful spirit, but I
knew there would be a lot of intense feeling at the service.
Both of Jon's parents, who were divorced, would be there,
along with many of his past lovers and a very diverse group
of people. And I knew that Jon's sister had just lost her own
little girl to a tragic death, and that the family had gone
through more pain in the past few years than most families
do in a lifetime.

The service was held in the home of Jon's mother. His partner had decorated the entire house with huge yellow sun-
flowers, Jon's favorite. Pictures of Jon were displayed everywhere. Over a hundred of us crowded into the living room,

and as Jon's favorite music played in the background, I began by sharing these words:

> *"Many traditions believe that at the time of passing on, the soul has a chance to evaluate its life and its choices, and that a gathering together of those who loved him will help the soul see his value, celebrate himself and, wrapped in love, go on toward the Light and the beautiful adventure that awaits."*

Suddenly, I could feel the relief in the room as we all realized that our purpose in coming together was to celebrate Jon, not to mourn him. The death of a loved one leaves those who are still alive feeling so powerless, and at a loss as to what to do with all the feelings that can no longer be shared directly with that person. But as we sat close together on that special evening, **each of us felt purposeful, even in our grief, for we knew we could do something—we could love.**

And that is what we did. We spent several hours loving Jon, through sharing cherished experiences, telling funny stories, remembering the fabulous food he cooked for his customers and his friends, and acknowledging how he had touched our lives. We laughed, we cried, we prayed for the peaceful journey of his spirit. And when it was all over, we each lit a floating candle and placed it in the swimming pool as we said our special good-byes.

Driving home by myself that night, I thanked Jon for the priceless gift he had given me by allowing me to facilitate the celebration of his passing. I had been reminded, once again, of the healing power of love:

> When we bring enough love into the darkness,
> it will illuminate our hearts with light
> and soothe our pain.

> When we bring enough love to our difficult
> times, it will reward us with real moments.

✦

There are times like these when, for just a moment, we open our hearts and share the best of ourselves. *We remember how to love.* Just after the big earthquake in January 1994, I stood trembling on the street outside my house in Los Angeles. Neighbors in bathrobes offered one another food, comfort, and extra batteries—it reminded me of Woodstock, or the gatherings I used to attend in the late 1960s. For a few days, we of so many races and dialects in Los Angeles were one family. You could feel the love. And then the intensity of the crisis was over. And the love went away.

Why does it take tragedy and difficult times to bring us back to love? Why do we need nature's close calls to make us realize how much we love our mates, our children, our friends? Why do we forget to love until it is too late? How much pain and destruction will it take for us to remember?

There is a beautiful portion of *A Course in Miracles* which reads:

> "Trials are but lessons that you failed to learn, presented once again."

I often wonder whether we would have fewer difficult times if we remembered to share more love and find more real moments during the easy days.

Perhaps crisis forces us to return to our center when we have drifted away from our true values, and to put our lives in perspective when we have forgotten what is really important. . . .

Perhaps it is the Universe's way of getting our attention fast, and refocusing us on love. . . .

Perhaps this is the hidden gift that difficult times hold for us.

✦

My wish for you is that you have
many happy days,
and few sorrows. But when those
difficult times come,
may you meet them with surrender,
and move through them with love.

Part Three

REAL MOMENTS
AND RELATIONSHIPS

·

· 7 ·

REAL MOMENTS
AND LOVING

"There is only one path to Heaven. On Earth, we call it Love."
— KAREN GOLDMAN

Of all the wonders life on Earth has to offer, none is greater to me than Love. Love infuses life with meaning. It performs magic and miracles. It brings light where there was darkness and hope where there was despair. It is your greatest teacher, and your most constant blessing.

Love is a force more formidable than any other. It is invisible—it cannot be seen, nor measured, yet it is powerful enough to transform you in a moment, and offer you more joy than any material possession could. Once love is yours, no one can take it away from you. Only you can relinquish it, if you wish.

Love is the magician of the Universe. It creates everything out of nothing. One moment, it isn't there, and the next— POOF—it appears in all its splendor, and you greet it with amazement. And what delights it produces out of thin air— smiles, laughter, goose bumps, hot flashes, tender words, silly names, happy tears, and, most of all, life. Love produced you. Without it, you wouldn't be here at all.

Love's greatest gift is its ability
to make everything it touches sacred.

Love sanctifies life. *Where love is, you are given a glimpse of the sacred.* You rise above your humanness and see the world through heavenly eyes. Your child, your beloved, your dog or cat, your garden, or whatever it is that you love appears adorable, precious, supremely beautiful, and somehow perfect in spite of its imperfections. And love also consecrates time and place and possession, bestowing special stature upon them: The day you first met your husband; the anniversary of your wedding; the special bench in the park where you go to talk; the rocking chair in which you nursed your child; the old afghan your grandmother made you; your little girl's first note that said "I love you, Mommy"; these become sacred artifacts commemorating the presence of love in your life.

But most of all, I believe that love offers you an opportunity for deep, spiritual awakening, for when you love, the usual boundaries which separate you from something else dissolve; you transcend the illusion of separation which defines human existence, and you experience Oneness. Suddenly, you are no longer alone in the Universe. There is a flow between your being and the being of whomever you are loving. All that is you is pouring out into them, and all that is them is pouring out into you. Your souls are dancing together.

Perhaps you have had moments like this, but not known exactly why they moved you so much. . . .

You and your husband stand above the crib of your newborn child, watching her sleep. Her tiny body rises and falls with the rhythm of her peaceful breathing, and you turn to your husband and his eyes meet yours. All at once, you feel a force of love circling from you to him to your daughter and back to you again, and as you flow in the fullness of the en-

ergy, you are aware of a timeless bond that connects you together. Nothing else exists. You feel totally complete.

✦

It's late at night and you're sitting outside on your back
porch listening to the crickets and watching the stars. Your
faithful dog who's been your best friend for ten years pads up
alongside of you, and nuzzles his head under your arm. As
you hold his warm body close to yours, you suddenly feel a
surge of love for him, and the unconditional devotion he has
always shown you. He raises his head and, for a long moment,
looks at you as if to say, "Yes, I feel it too." The night swallows
both of you up into an eternal peace, and it seems you are the
only two beings in the world. This moment is all yours.

This is the power of love—*it takes you on a journey from
separation to Oneness.* It penetrates the normal boundaries in
which you live, the boundaries that make you feel like "you,"
distinct and unrelated to anyone or anything else. You know
that you are not your husband or wife or dog or friend or the
sky. And yet, in those very real moments of love, "you" turns
into "us," something infinitely more fulfilling than you alone.

In this way, love creates an unlimited experience with no
boundaries, no edges. It allows you to travel out of yourself.

All love is an out-of-body experience.

You may not have ever considered yourself a spiritual person,
but every true experience of love is spiritual, as your spirit
touches the spirit of someone or something else. **Love becomes your doorway into the divine.**

*Love is the ultimate method for creating real moments, be-
cause love forces you to practice mindfulness.* It pulls you into
an eternal present. It focuses all of your attention on what
you are experiencing, and it requires that you surrender to it.

The better you become at loving, the more real moments you will be able to create.

✦

"Every deep love relationship is a path of initiation, a journey involving many tests and trials."
— BARRY AND JOYCE VISSEL

An intimate relationship is a sacred opportunity for you to use love as a path for personal and spiritual transformation. It forces you to open where you were closed, to feel where you were numb, to express what was silent, to reach out where you would retreat. *It's easy to feel like you are a loving and enlightened person when you are alone, but when you get into a relationship, you come face-to-face with every emotional limitation you possess.*

Relationships are an instant and continual training ground. They insist that you look in the mirror at yourself, they reveal all the parts of you that are not loving. They show you your dark side. They knock on the door of your heart, demanding that you open the places you've kept locked. And then, every day and night, they give you an opportunity to practice love, to stretch yourself beyond what is comfortable, and to keep doing it better.

Using Your Relationship as a Path

I chose to follow the path of love at a very early age, for I knew it would lead me to the real moments of meaning I was searching for. It has been an exciting, mysterious, often painful but always liberating journey. For a long time, I wasn't very good at loving. I made many mistakes; I hurt myself and I hurt others. But slowly, I learned how to use love and relationship as a sacred path of learning and transformation. And

I was finally blessed to find a man who was willing to travel that same path with me, and share the adventure.

All great creations begin with a vision. Before an artist paints, he has a vision of the picture in his mind. Before an architect designs a building, she has a vision of what it should look like. Before a musician writes a piece of music, he hears the finished piece in his head. Vision fuels the birth of all that is produced with love.

> If you don't have a vision of where you want
> your relationship to go, it won't go anywhere.

Being in a relationship without both of you agreeing on its destination is like trying to take a long road trip without a map—you're going to get lost over and over again, and you're not going to enjoy the ride. To use your relationship as a path, both you and your partner must create a shared vision of the purpose of your being together, and then make a sincere commitment to living that vision.

Vision helps us get through difficult times. It focuses our awareness on the destination, and encourages us to keep going, even when we feel lost or disheartened. It is the vision of the career you want to have that helps you study, write papers, and work hard through college. It is the vision of holding your newborn baby in your arms that gives you, as a mother, courage to get through the pain of labor. **It is the vision of your relationship as a transformational path that will give you and your partner the strength, patience, and perseverance to travel the High Road of Love together.**

Here are several truths that make up the vision my husband and I share of our relationship:

1. We have been brought together for the purpose of helping each other grow, and will be each other's teacher.

2. Our relationship is a precious gift—it will take us through whatever we need to learn to become more conscious, loving human beings.

3. The challenges and difficulties we experience will always illuminate our most needed lessons.

Because we have made a commitment to accept this purposeful vision of our love, we experience the struggles and problems we encounter in a sacred context. When we argue, we are angry at one another, when we get frustrated and feel like turning away, our vision shines like a beacon of light in the fog, reminding us that there is a higher purpose to the everyday difficulties we're challenged by. *We remember that we have chosen to travel together for a reason, and by remembering, we can more quickly release the anger, move beyond the hurt, forgive, and find our eternal bond of love that is always present underneath.*

It is easy to forget the true purpose of your relationship when you are busy with work, children, and family obligations. And when you forget your purpose as a couple, you lose your way. A relationship that has lost its way will stop moving and growing, for it won't know where it is supposed to go.

If you and your partner have lost your way, seek out real moments together. In them, you will find your way back home to the heart of your love.

Feeding the Soul of Your Relationship

You need real moments of intimacy, of oneness, to nourish the spirit of your love so that it will continue to grow. Sharing these moments with your partner reminds you both of your timeless connection, your purpose in finding one another, and thus gives you renewed vision and courage to get you through the challenges of living together.

Real moments are the life blood of intimate relationships.

Without real moments, the soul of your relationship will die. You may still choose to ignore your lack of fulfillment and stay together, but your relationship will exist as an empty shell, an arrangement of convenience you make in order not to be alone.

Having real moments of intimacy doesn't mean just being with someone. It's what *happens* when you are together that makes it a real moment of love. You can be physically together and be emotionally a million miles away because you are not in the moment. Or you can create a real moment on the phone, even though you're calling from 1,000 miles away, simply because you are letting the boundaries go and sharing the deepest parts of your heart.

Most relationships I see around me are suffering from real-moment deprivation. It's not that the two people don't love each other—they do. But *they don't feel the love as deeply as they should,* because they aren't giving the love opportunities to surface and be experienced without distraction. *They aren't having enough real moments together.*

✦

Earlier this year, my husband and I spent/an hour with a wonderful woman named Robin, picking out our wedding invitations. Jeffrey left her store first to get back to his office, and I stayed to finish up the details.

"He's wonderful!" Robin remarked. "You two make a great couple. You seem like best friends, and I loved watching you interact together."

"Thank you," I answered. "Believe me, we've worked really hard to get our relationship to be as good as it is."

"Do you want to hear something sad? I must see twenty couples a week who come in here to pick out invitations, and I'd say on a good week, maybe one couple actually seems to be happy together, and behaves lovingly toward each other. It makes me wonder why they're even getting married."

Robin's comment didn't surprise me. I know from teaching seminars for so many years that her observation is sad but true. Most people look at a relationship like a possession—"I have a car; I have a job; I have a relationship." The relationship becomes something to *get*, and once that goal has been obtained, they don't put much time or energy into it.

Marriage is not a noun, it's a verb. It isn't something you get, it's something you do.

Marriage is not a wedding ring, or a piece of paper that proves you are husband and wife, or a party that says you've been married for twenty-five years. Marriage is a *behavior*—it is how you love and honor your partner every day. You aren't married because the county or your family thinks you are. *The real act of marriage takes place in the heart,* not in ballroom or a church or a synagogue. It is a choice you make, not just on your wedding day, but over and over again, and that choice is reflected in the way you treat your husband or wife.

Your marriage is renewed and reconsecrated every time you share a real moment together.

✦

"Every moment of your life,
you are offered the opportunity to choose—love or fear—
to tread the earth, or to soar the heavens.
Fear would walk you on a narrow path,
promising to take you where you want to go.
Love says, 'Open your arms and fly with me.' "
— EMMANUEL, as told by Pat Rodegast

We avoid real moments in relationships because if we aren't used to them, they can be frightening in their intensity:
Have you ever sat with someone you loved late at night, sharing your thoughts, your hopes, your secret feelings? At first, you're just talking, but at some point, enough doors have been opened, enough connection has been made, and something greater than your two individual selves is created. It is tangible. You both can feel it. It is a space you occupy together, a sacred space that emerges when enough truth has been spoken, and acknowledged. Suddenly, you feel your connectedness as strong as anything you've ever felt. You are experiencing a real moment.

All at once you realize that you are out of control. Your boundaries have melted, and the usual protections you have are dissolving, leaving you uncomfortable in your vulnerability. You are being seen without your masks, your innermost emotions are being witnessed by someone else. The sanctity of your personal space has been penetrated.

Ironically, this is actually the definition of love, when you allow your soul to touch someone else's. If you are not good at trusting and letting go, you will pull away from the moment, and turn away from the love, for fear that you will lose yourself in it. You will crave retreat from your partner, maybe even from the relationship. Or perhaps you will just avoid intimacy and relationship entirely, knowing that without it, those terrifying moments of vulnerability cannot happen.

What are you running from? Your own nakedness. What are you afraid of? Losing your edges, your ego, and being swallowed up by a force more powerful than you. It is a kind of death—the death of your separateness, the death of your illusions about yourself.

Many of us spend our life playing hide-and-seek with ourselves—we do whatever we can to avoid facing our truth, and exploring our shadows. *If this has been your agenda, you will be terrified of true, deep love and the real moments of surrender it requires of you.* And you will find ways to flee from them.

Clarissa Pinkola Estés, author of *Women Who Run with the Wolves*, says that: "Fear is a poor excuse for not doing the work. We are all afraid. It is nothing new. If you are alive, you are fearful . . . **To love means to stay when every cell says run!**"

Loving may appear to be an emotional risk, but in reality, it isn't a risk at all.

You never lose by loving.
You always lose by holding back love.

. , . The real risk is in living with someone year after year without truly knowing their soul, or their knowing yours.

. . . The real risk is having a marriage based on materialism and superficiality, and avoiding those kinds of human connection that are truly significant.

. . . *The real risk is being in a relationship without real moments.*

Finding Your Ability to Feel Again

Experiencing intimacy with your beloved requires that you open yourself totally to the moment, not just by showing up physically, but by *showing up emotionally*. You aren't pretending to listen, but thinking about something else; you aren't reading the paper while she is trying to reach out; you aren't going through the motions of loving, but feeling numb—you are fully present with him or with her. After all, if *you* aren't *there* in the moment, then who is there to love, to connect, to be intimate with?

Being there emotionally in the moment means knowing how to fully feel your feelings.

The ability to feel love is based on the *ability to feel* . . . period. *You can't feel love or happiness or contentment if you have forgotten how to feel.* Many of us were robbed of our ability to feel as children. Now, as adults, not feeling has become an old habit—we suppress, edit, and deny our emotions on a regular basis. We respond to requests for connection with phrases like: *"Not now," "I don't want to talk about it," "Nothing's wrong," "Aren't you ever satisfied?"* We drink alcohol, take drugs, eat junk food, work incessantly, and watch too much TV, all in an attempt to numb ourselves. Thus we carry years of frozen feelings inside of our hearts, and when it comes time to connect, to be intimate, even if we want to, we don't know how.

> Finding your ability to feel again is the first
> step toward experiencing true intimacy with your
> partner and creating real moments
> in relationship.

To do this, you need to defrost the ice around your heart. Cry all the tears you never shed; release the old rage from your body; find your voice and give it permission to say all the things it has kept silent for so long. *The more you work on healing your emotional wounds, the easier it will be for you to love.*

I've spent my whole life developing powerful and effective

techniques to break down emotional walls. I needed them first to heal myself, and then to share with my students. There are many other teachers and therapists who also offer their own methods for emotional healing. **Use us. We are here to help you find your way back to yourself.**

✦

"You learn to speak by speaking, to study by studying, to run by running, to work by working; and just so, you learn to love . . . by loving. All those who think to learn in any other way deceive themselves."

— SAINT FRANCIS DE SALES

How do you begin to experience more real moments in loving? **You begin.** No putting it off until your next vacation, or Saturday night, or until you finish this chapter. *Now* is the time. No waiting until it feels right, or until you think you'll be better at it. *It will never feel right until you do it, and you won't get better at it until you start.*

Loving well is a skill, just like playing an instrument, or operating a computer, or cooking—the more you do it, the better you get. Creating real moments of intimacy takes practice. You could listen to every tape I've recorded, or attend every seminar on relationships that is available, but you still wouldn't be good at loving. **Loving is the only way to get good at loving.**

Many years ago, before I even became a teacher, I was married to a well-known magician. He was a master at creating exquisite illusions on stage and doing miraculous sleight of hand with coins and cards. Whenever anyone would ask him how he made his magic look so effortless, he would explain that he'd spent years practicing, and he'd share his favorite saying:

"The difficult must become habit, the habit easy, and the easy beautiful."

It's been over fifteen years since I've heard that phrase, but as I write today, I haven't been able to get it out of my mind. It *is* difficult to love well, but the more we work on it, loving becomes a habit. You no longer have to remind yourself to tell your partner how much you appreciate him—you just find yourself doing it; he doesn't have to be asked to share his feelings—he volunteers them on his own. Suddenly, it feels more natural for you both to love, to give, to open, than it does to not love and to hold back. And the more you each give, the easier it gets, until there's no more effort. Finally, what's become easy begins to deepen as you and your beloved step out of the way and allow love to simply flow through each of you to the other. Your love has become beautiful.

✦

In the first section of this book, I said happiness is a choice, and so is love.

<blockquote>Love is a choice you make from
moment to moment.</blockquote>

You *choose* to love, to express it, to share it, to show it. You do not wait to be seized by an overwhelming feeling of love that propels you into action. You don't wait to say "I love you" until the words are bursting out of your mouth. You don't wait to give your wife a hug until you can't physically control yourself. *You make these gestures because you remember that you love this person, and because you know that by choosing to love, you will not only make your partner happy, but you will focus your own attention on the love you feel and bring yourself joy.*

Creating Real Moments in Your Relationship

Real moments will not chase you down as you race busily through your life. *You must invite them into your relationship by setting aside the time and space in which they can occur.*

- ✦ Set your alarm clock to go off ten minutes earlier so you can cuddle in bed
- ✦ Meet for a picnic lunch in a park
- ✦ Take a silent walk holding hands
- ✦ Go for a long drive to nowhere
- ✦ Sit together on the couch by candlelight
- ✦ Share your deepest fears and wildest dreams
- ✦ Turn off the television, start talking, and see what happens

Many couples insulate themselves from the intimacy of real moments by always having other people around—their children, their relatives, their friends. They rarely go out together alone. They use the excuse of being there for the kids to avoid each other. And when they do take a vacation, it is always with one or two other couples. Does this sound familiar to you? I hope not, because it is a dangerous way to live. You will wake up one day, look at your partner, and see the face of a stranger.

You need to be selfish in order to have real moments together. Do whatever it takes to find the time. And don't worry about neglecting your children or your friends. They will feel your renewed love and rejoice in it.

The greatest gift you and your partner can give
your children is the example of an intimate,
healthy, and loving relationship.

✦

Every couple must follow their own road to their own real moments. But here are some things that can help if you're not sure where to begin.

Feeding Your Partner's Heart—The "3 × 3 Formula"

Most people I see are walking around **love-starved**. Their hearts are hungry for love, and they aren't getting enough. Ask yourself right now:

"Am I getting enough love from my partner?"

"Is my partner getting enough love from me?"

I've developed an *Intimacy Formula* to help you feed your partner's heart: Our bodies need to eat three meals a day, with a few snacks in between. Our hearts needs to be nourished in the same way. **Feeding your partner's heart means feeding him/her three Love Meals a day. That means three times a day when you choose to actively love your partner, for at least three minutes.** I call this the "3 × 3 Formula," three minutes of intimacy three times a day to feed your partner's heart. Maybe it's three minutes in the morning together before you get out of bed, three minutes on the phone in the middle of the day, and three minutes after the kids go to sleep.

But Love Meals aren't enough—your partner also needs little **love snacks.** A love snack is a kiss on the neck, a compliment, a note you leave him, a thank-you, a phone call to say "I love you." Love snacks may only take a few seconds, but they create instant connection, and *mini-real moments.*

What do you feed your partner during these Love Meals and Love Snacks? Just like we have the four basic food groups in nutrition, I've come up with three basic emotional food groups, that I call **The Three A's: Attention, Affection, and Appreciation.** You *pay* attention, you *show affection,* and you *express appreciation.* When you give your mate these three ingredients during your three minutes, you will be nourishing his or her heart.

Attention: *Paying attention means being there 100 percent, totally in the moment with the person you love.* You are not doing anything else other than being there for them. When you give your partner all of your attention, even for a few moments, they have the opportunity to really feel you, and to receive your love. Look into their eyes; ask yourself what they need from you. You already know the answer. Remember—it is when we fully pay attention that real moments can occur.

Affection: *Showing affection means giving physical intimacy—touching, holding, being physically close together.* This kind of affection is not particularly sexual. Rather, it is loving. Physical affection soothes and heals our body and soul. It's even been shown to strengthen our immune system. It will help connect you and your partner emotionally by linking you on the physical dimension first.

Appreciation: *Expressing appreciation means demonstrating your love verbally, telling your partner what you love about them, what you're grateful to them for, what they've done that has made you proud.* Most of us don't get enough appreciation, and are starving for gratitude. Notice that I did not say *showing* your appreciation by doing something, like making the bed for your wife, or getting your husband's car washed. This part of the formula needs to be verbal. You need to say the words: "Thank you for being so patient with me this morning when I was in a bad mood." "I am so proud of you for getting that new account at work." "I love the way you made our son feel so special for getting all A's and B's on his report card—you're really a great mom."

Three times a day, for at least three minutes, use the Three A's to feed your partner's heart. You will be amazed at the results. You will see your mate begin to glow right before your eyes. You will feel more in love. And you will have many more real moments.

Don't forget those Love Snacks. Ever since I came up with this whole concept, Jeffrey and I have been practicing it diligently, and several times a day, one of us will approach the other with a smile and announce: "Love Snack!" That's our cue for a quick hug or kiss. When any of our friends see us do this, and we explain how it works, invariably the wife will turn to her husband and say, "Hey, I want a Love Snack too!"

The purpose of this Intimacy Formula is to get you in the habit of having real moments of love and connection with your partner. It may sound like a cute little idea, but the effect it can have on your relationship is transformational.

Love Processes

Here are some structured ways of expressing your love called "Love Processes" that can create instant intimacy and real moments. You use these processes when you and your partner are alone together and have some uninterrupted quality time. It's helpful to sit across from one another, or next to each other, and hold hands. In each Love Process, you and your partner take turns going back and forth, each of you saying the key phrase, and then filling in the blank. The more specific you are in your response, the more powerful the exercise will be. After you are finished with one phrase, your partner should respond by thanking you, and then take his turn.

Here are a few examples for each Love Process. Your responses will probably be longer than these samples. You can spend as much time as you like doing a particular exercise. I suggest a minimum of ten minutes, and even longer is better.

The Appreciation Processes

◆ "Something I love about you is . . ."

"Something I love about you is how attentive you always are to me when I come home from work, making me feel like I can relax and let myself be taken care of for a while." (Thank you.)

"Something I love about you is what a great sense of humor you have—you always make me laugh when I'm being too serious, and I need that!" (Thank you.)

"Something I love about you is how hard you work on this relationship, and how much you reach out to me when I try to shut down. You never give up on me and you make it safe for me to open up." (Thank you.)

◆ "I love you because . . ."

"I love you because you always listen to my feelings, even when I know it's uncomfortable, and you make me feel like what I have to say is important." (Thank you.)

"I love you because you believe in me and my dreams for our family, and no one has stood by me before in my life like you have." (Thank you.)

"I love you because when I watch you play with our children, I see the little girl inside of you come out, and she is the sweetest, most loving person in the world."

The Gratitude Process

◆ "I'm grateful to you for . . ."

"I'm grateful to you for accepting my daughter as your own when we decided to get married, and being the father she never had." (Thank you.)

"I'm grateful to you for not giving up on us when I was so afraid of making a commitment, and helping me learn to trust love again. You saved my life." (Thank you.)

"I'm grateful to you for being so patient with me while I worked out my anger at my ex-husband, and loving me even when I took it out on you." (Thank you.)

The Forgiveness Process

✦ *"I'm sorry . . ."*

"I'm sorry that I make it so difficult for you to get through to me sometimes, and that I go so far away from you. I don't mean to make you work so hard to love me. I just get scared. *Please forgive me.*"

"I'm sorry that I criticized your ideas for remodeling the house last week, and made you feel like you weren't doing anything right. I'm so sorry I was so thoughtless, and didn't see how much you wanted to make things better for us. *Please forgive me.*"

"I'm sorry that I don't always let you know how much I need you, and get so busy with work that you feel neglected. I'm sorry I don't tell you every day that you're the most important thing in my life. *Please forgive me.*"

✦

I have seen these Love Processes create miracles in thousands of relationships, including my own. They work because they open the doors to your heart, and allow the love that has been waiting there to flow out, and, at the same time, invite your partner's love to flow in. I hope they lead you to many real and treasured moments together.

Making the Choice to Love Now

It is an unfortunate part of our human nature that we take what we have for granted until we lose it, and then weep for what can no longer be ours, and berate ourselves for the time we wasted.

If you have someone special in your life, don't wait to start loving them.

Do not put it off for even one day. Make the choice to love now. You do not, as your mind would like you to believe, have all the time in the world. Whoever loves you is only on loan from God, and he or she could be taken from you at any moment. I don't say this to frighten you. Believe me, I don't like this setup either. But that is the way it works, and why it is so important to make every day of loving count.

Let me share two stories with you. On the surface, they are both about death, but their real message is about life.

In Memory of Bobby

About eight years ago, I was teaching my Making Love Work weekend seminar in Los Angeles as I used to do each month. One of the course participants was a very successful man in his fifties. He'd accumulated great wealth over the course of his life by working eighteen hours a day. In the process, however, he had neglected his wife and three sons, and now, after twenty-five years of marriage, she was asking for a divorce. This man was devastated—he thought he'd been a good husband and father, and couldn't understand what he had done wrong. Even his therapist, who'd sent him to my course, hadn't been able to get through to him.

For two days in the seminar, this man did something he'd

never done in his life—he looked inward. There, deep within his heart, he found feelings he didn't know he'd had: love he had never expressed to his wife and sons; anger at his father for driving him to be successful from the time he was a small child; and tremendous grief that he was discovering all of this when it was already too late to salvage his relationship. For the first time since he was a little boy, he wept. On Saturday night, he shared that although he had failed in his marriage, he was determined to start new, caring relationships with his sons. "I can't wait to tell them how much I love them," he announced triumphantly, and we all cheered for his powerful breakthrough.

The next morning, just after we began our session, one of my staff members interrupted the class with an emergency. "There's a woman and her two sons in the lobby," she whispered. "They need to find their father who's taking the class. It seems that their brother was killed early this morning in a bicycling accident in Europe."

I caught my breath. Right away, I knew who the man they sought was. We escorted him out of the room, and then we all held each other as we heard his sobs and screams of anguish when his wife told him the tragic news. Suddenly, the door opened, and he approached the stage and asked me if he could address the group before he left.

I will never forget that moment as long as I live. He stood before us, tears streaming down his face: "I want to say two things," he began. "First, I thank God that I was here this weekend, because I learned how to feel, and if I hadn't gone through this seminar, I wouldn't even have been able to cry for my son. I would have been numb like I've been my whole life.

"And second, you all know how excited I was about the future, about finally being able to tell my boys how much I loved them, how proud I was of them. But now I'll never be able to tell Bobby that, because he's gone. I lost my chance. So please, if I can give you anything, let it be this: *Don't wait until it's too late, like I did. If there are people in your life who you love, tell them, show them, and do it today. Because you don't know if they will still be here tomorrow.*"

All of us in that room wept along with our friend as the truth he spoke penetrated our hearts. Our minds turned to our own husbands and wives and brothers and fathers and children we took for granted, assuming they would still be alive by the time we got around to telling them how much we loved them.

As the man turned to leave, I made him a promise—that Bobby's death would not be in vain, that I would share this story whenever I could for the rest of my life, as a reminder for whoever heard it to *love now.* So this was for you, Bobby. . . .

In Memory of Ellen

Ellen Baron was my rabbi's wife, and my friend. She died three years ago after a long and painful battle with cancer. Ellen was my age. At the time of her death, she was forty years old, and her son, Jonathan, was five.

When I first met Ellen, it was hard to imagine that she had cancer, because she was so physically beautiful. She had a radiance about her that was impossible to miss. She exuded life and love, and we all were sure that if anyone could conquer the disease, Ellen could.

Ellen's strong and courageous spirit did conquer her cancer, as she used it to move into even higher levels of consciousness and propel her through tremendous personal transformation. But Ellen's body could not fight off the physical assault of the disease, and after years of agonizing treatment, she knew it was time to go, and she passed on.

No death is ever welcome, but Ellen's illness and death seemed especially incomprehensible. She and David, her husband, were a rare couple completely in love with each other, and in her support for his work as a rabbi, her kindness and gentle spirit touched thousands of people every year. When she died, those who loved her were devastated.

Ellen's funeral was a standing-room-only affair. One by one, Ellen's many friends, her doctors, her son, and her husband got up to share their cherished memories, their pain, their loss, and, more than anything else, their love with all of us, and with Ellen's spirit which we could feel hovering nearby. For several hours, with laughter and with tears, we celebrated the woman that had been Ellen Baron, and acknowledged her passing into a different form.

I remember at one point looking around the chapel and seeing everyone, even strangers, holding hands with each other. The love in the room was overpowering. Suddenly, an enormous wave of sadness washed over me. *"Why do we wait until the people we love die to celebrate them?"* I asked myself. *"Why is the day on which we love and honor a person the most, a day when he or she can no longer hear our words? Why don't we share those stories and memories and feelings with the same depth of passion while that person is living?'*

Ellen should have been standing before us, surrounded by baskets of flowers, as we paid tribute to the magnificent wife, mother, and woman she was. She had always been well loved, but I couldn't help thinking that it took death to finally put her fully in the spotlight.

Do the people in your life really know how much you love them, and how deeply you need them? Don't wait to celebrate them until they pass from the earth. Don't save up your words for their funeral. Don't put off loving them with abandon. **Do it now.**

Give a "life party" for someone you love. Invite that person's friends, family, and neighbors, and allow each of them to take turns sharing their appreciation and gratitude.

We need to start memorializing life instead of death, and create real moments today, rather than real memories tomorrow.

✦

"The distinction between human and spiritual is made only by human beings. They are not separate. They are woven together. If you do not open your heart to human beings, you will find it difficult to open your heart to God. If you do not love human beings, including yourself, you will find it difficult to love God. Your spiritual path begins in your humanness, with the simple day-to-day willingness to be honest, kind, and loving, to the best of your ability."
— RON SCOLASTICO AND THE GUIDES

Ultimately, loving is a spiritual practice. When you love a person, or an animal, or a tree, you are loving a piece of God. And each real moment in loving gives you a chance to bring the sacred into form, and, thus, participate in creating a little more Heaven on earth.

Look around you—
you will see someone who needs your love.
Offer it to them,
In that moment, you will be their blessing.
And God will be smiling.

∗ 8 ∗

WOMEN AND
REAL MOMENTS

> "O Great Mother, mother of us all, oldest of the old,
> come to me through the labyrinth of time
> to help me remember the wisdom of my forebears,
> the eternal life-giving power of woman."
> — HALLIE IGLEHARD AUSTEN

I write this chapter as a woman, to you who are also women, so that we may find the real moments we need to nourish ourselves. I write this too for all men who love women and seek to understand us.

Women, you see, know about real moments in the very core of our being. *Real moments are our natural territory.* We are at home with them, like a bird that catches the wind and allows it to take her wherever it is going. *Flying requires surrender, and that is why women are so good at soaring through the valleys and canyons of our inner world—we understand how to surrender.* Our bodies are made for it. We surrender when we make love, and receive our beloved. We surrender each month to our moon cycles, and release the blood which we do not need. We surrender during childbirth and allow our son or daughter to emerge into the world. And when we let ourselves, we surrender easily into real moments.

Women are alchemists.
We transmute the ordinary into the miraculous.

We can make a walk down the street with our child an enchanted adventure. We can take an empty room, put some plants here, some curtains there, and make it into a place that feels like home. We know how to turn a quiet conversation with the person we love into an opportunity for true communion. We can transform the simple act of arranging flowers, wrapping a gift, or giving a hug into a sacred moment filled with feeling. Herein lies our power, as well as that which frightens men most about us—*we see the potential for magic and love in everything.*

Since the beginning of time, and until recently, women have had more access to real moments than men simply because of the way our roles in the world were structured. Society would not let us out, and so we turned inward. We stayed at home with our children. We had more quiet, more solitude, more moments of connection. We baked bread and worked in our gardens, we read, we knitted, we prayed.

In this past century, we have gained our freedom to live as equals with men, but in the process, we've lost our spiritual center. We have taken on men's stress-related diseases, men's physical and emotional exhaustion, men's lack of peace. Our freedom is killing us. We are missing our real moments. And we desperately need to get them back.

✦

Women are the nurturers and givers of the world—we are genetically and psychologically programmed to take care of everyone. We can tune in to another person's needs before he can. We know when our baby is about to cry. We know when our husband needs to cry. If someone sneezes, we offer them a tissue. If someone is angry, we offer them a smile. We want to do whatever it takes to make everyone happy. We are pleasers. We love to love.

The problem is that when we make pleasing others a priority, we often do it at the price of neglecting to please ourselves. By being so self-sacrificing, we deprive ourselves of the time and opportunity to have the very real moments we seek and are so good at savoring. *We become disconnected from the core of who we are.*

Do you know what the worst thing you can call a woman is? **SELFISH.** . . . Most of us would rather be called anything than that. Call me a wimp, a pushover, a coward, a love addict, but don't call me selfish. Selfish means I am not thinking of your needs. Selfish means I'm not taking care of you. Selfish means I am a bitch. Selfish means I am not a woman.

We are taught from the time we are little girls that to be loving means to take everyone else's feelings into account. No father says to their daughter, as they do to their sons, "Go out there and kick ass, honey. Make them all look like nothing compared to you." Instead we are told to be nice, to share, to understand, to apologize, to forgive. These are good behaviors. Men need to practice more of these. *But as women, we do these too much.* We give when we should insist on receiving. We forgive when we should state our ultimatum. We apologize when we should demand an apology.

> Women need real moments of solitude and
> self-reflection to balance out how much of
> ourselves we give away.

For women, taking the time for real moments is a matter of psychological and spiritual survival. If we do not, we will be sucked dry by everyone and everything that needs us. We need to create a day, an hour, even five minutes, when we give to ourselves only, and not to anyone else. We need to regularly replenish our generous spirits, so we can continue to give without resentment and without emotional burnout. We need silence. We need space. We need to listen to the pleas of our own heart, and no other.

But let us confess the truth—we are not good at this, at being self-ish. We are uncomfortable doing things just for ourselves. *It makes us feel guilty.* We suspect we are abandoning everyone, the husband, the kids, the dog, the friend in crisis. And so we feel the need to apologize when we take care of ourselves, whether it's going off for a day alone, or closing the door and reading for two hours, or attending a class and leaving the family with take-out food. "Look, I'll only be gone for four hours, and when I come back, I'll play games with you all night, O.K.?" "Honey, I know I'm leaving you with a lot to do when I go away to visit my friend, but I'll make lists of everything." Bribery, submissive behavior, we'll do anything—just don't be mad at us for leaving you.

Men have no problem being selfish, and I say this with admiration, at least in this context. If they want to ignore the family after dinner and read the paper, they do it. They don't apologize, they don't keep sneaking glances at you to see if you're "O.K." with their decision. They forget about you and everyone else. Why then, as women, are we compelled to make excuses when we nourish ourselves? Why do we feel we need to "make up" for our real moments alone by giving twice as much when we return?

> To have real moments and find your center
> again, you have to stop worrying about what
> other people think.

If you have been giving on command and living selflessly, some people in your life who have come to depend on you for their emotional sustenance, moral support, car pooling, regular meals, clean laundry, free advice, and whatever else you've been handing out will probably not like it very much when you start taking time for you. They may openly express their displeasure, or they may just get grumpy. Ignore them. They will get used to your special personal times, even encourage them, once they see the new light in your eyes and feel the new calm in your heart.

Even before I began writing this book, I realized I wasn't having enough real moments with myself. Over the course of a few months, I made some dramatic changes in how I was spending my time. I gave up teaching many of the regular seminars people had always relied upon. I stopped going out to social events I wasn't interested in. And now, as I am in the middle of my writing process, I'm not even answering my phone, but having my assistant inform people that I'm in seclusion until the book is done. This is sure upsetting some of my friends and acquaintances. It's hard for them to believe that I am not there for them when *they* want me to be, which is the story of my life. Of course, no one has come out and actually said: "How dare you take time for yourself, you selfish bitch," but I can feel a few of them thinking it.

And how am I feeling? Absolutely wonderful. I am coming back into balance. Having given and given and given some more, I desperately needed to replenish my own source of inner sustenance.

✦

"Is this then what happens to woman? She wants perpetually to spill herself away. All her instinct as a woman—the eternal nourisher of children, of men, of society—demands that she give. Her time, her energy, her creativeness drain out into these channels if there is any chance, any leak."
— ANNE MORROW LINDBERGH

Men are entities unto themselves. They know where their edges are, where they end and the world begins. But the boundaries between women and the world around us are not solid—they are permeable. Our edges are blurred, our perimeters porous, and through the holes, our spirit leaks out. *We are in a constant process of give and take with what is outside of us.*

Women are all moonchildren. Our bodies change with the cycles of the moon—it pulls on us, just as it does the ocean, creating invisible tides within our soul that no one else can see, but we can feel. *In this way our body is never completely our own.* Each month, it belongs to the moon. When I am pregnant, it belongs to my child—for three quarters of a year, someone else is actually living inside of me. After I give birth, it is not over—my breasts belong to my son or daughter as my milk flows forth to feed them.

In relationships too, we have been designed to be permeated—in order to join together sexually, it is I who must open myself and receive my lover. He enters inside of me, and with a part of himself, he touches a dark, hidden place that I cannot even touch myself. What before was me alone now includes another.

But it is not just our bodies that give and receive so naturally—it is our psyches as well. When we walk down the street, or walk into a room, or talk on the phone, we feel feelings that are not our own, and pick up on other people's angers, hurts, and yearnings we don't even want to know about. A child cries somewhere—a part of you leaps out psychically to hold it. There is a crisis or tragedy thousands of miles away—you find your day is ruined, because a part of you is there, comforting, helping. These are not decisions that we can control. They are instincts that are bred into our feminine fiber. Forces pull on us, and without thinking, we respond.

Our permeable nature is what makes women so wonderfully flexible, so able to heal quickly after defeat, so capable of picking ourselves up and starting over. *But we live in constant danger of becoming overly adaptive and overly responsive to what pulls on us from the outside, and thus being pulled off center and losing ourselves.*

Women need times when we close off our
borders to everything but ourselves.

We need moments when we shut all the doors of our being that are perpetually open and retreat within. *We need times when we are not physically, emotionally, or psychically accessible to anyone or anything but our own hungers and dreams and voices. We need real moments with ourselves.*

Close down the store for inventory. Don't worry about the customers. They'll be there when you open up for business again.

Gathering the Scatterings of Your Soul

Most women I know have spent their lives giving away pieces of themselves, one after the other. We give a piece to our lover, a piece to each of our children, pieces to friends, parents, in-laws, bosses, employees, committees, and just about anyone else who asks, and even those who don't. We scatter fragments of our soul around like careless offerings, and yet we are surprised, at some point, to find ourselves so empty and emotionally depleted, and we can't quite seem to figure out how it happened.

Coming into wholeness as a woman isn't so
much about discovering who you are, but about
taking back the parts of yourself you gave away.

If you think other people took your power from you, you can never get it back, because you never relinquished it. When you see that you gave your power away, then you can begin the process of retrieving it.

My real awakening as a woman began when I started the process of retrieving lost pieces of my Self. These were the scatterings of my soul, pieces of my integrity, my self-respect, my truth, my trust, that I had given to my father, my ex-husbands, my lovers, my employers, my gurus, my business partners. Some pieces I had given when I was just a child, hoping to be loved, hoping to keep Daddy from leaving, and when he left anyway, hoping to get him to come back once in a while. Some pieces I gave when I fell in love, hoping to avoid conflict, hoping to make everything look good, to make a man feel I was so perfect for him, he couldn't possibly choose someone else. Some pieces I gave away by not speaking up for myself when I should have, by pretending I had enough when I needed more, by crying when I should have shouted, by smiling when I should have walked away.

These are soul bribes. We barter pieces of our soul, and in the process, betray ourselves . . . but for what? So we can say we are in a relationship? So we have a ring to prove we are loved? So we don't have to be alone on Saturday night? So we can have a nice house and nice things, even though we're miserable? So our kids can have a father around, even if he is a real jerk?

Each woman has her price. Each of us is seduced into betraying herself by different temptations. For me, it has always been *belonging.* I used to pay any soul price to lovers, to friends, to teachers—anyone who would act like they were there for me, anyone who would stay. For many women, it is security. I can think of at least ten of my friends right now who are only staying with their husbands because they are so "comfortable," and don't want to give up their lifestyle. They are willing to live passionless, dishonest lives so they can still drive their nice car and keep their big house with the live-in maid.

I grieve for every woman who sells her soul and gives up her name just so she can feel like somebody. I grieve for every woman who is willing to change her values, her opinions, and even her breast size just so she can get a man to accept her. I grieve for all of us everywhere who have scattered our souls.

A time will come in your life when you cannot go forward without putting yourself back together. A time will come when you realize you can't achieve any kind of peace if you leave those orphaned parts of yourself behind. You suddenly awaken, and know you must go and gather the scatterings of your soul.

How do we do this? It is different for each of us. Some of us who have very little soul power left need to leave where we are and whom we are with in order to get ourselves back. Some of us need to stop running from love and settle down. Some of us need to start saying all the things we have been hiding to all the people we have been hiding the truth from. Some of us need to stop talking so much and start listening to our own silence. Some of us need to quit our jobs. Some of us need to get jobs. Some of us need to make new rules with everyone in our life. Some of us need to break the rules. Some of us need to shut the door, turn off the phone, and become a hermit for a while. Some of us need to get out of the house and stop hiding.

Slowly, piece by piece, we put ourselves together again. Each time I have brought a piece of myself back home to my heart, I have felt my soul rejoice, like a mother welcoming back a long-lost child. And with each new homecoming, I emerge into my life with more courage and less fear.

There is a story I have heard many times in many different versions about sticks. If you take one stick and try to break it, you can do it easily. But if you put that stick together with many others, and then try to break the sticks, you cannot do it. The bundle is too strong. A woman without her missing pieces is like a solitary stick. She can be easily broken. *But a woman with all the pieces of her soul bundled together has the power of wholeness, and is unbreakable.*

Letting Your Spirit Out to Run Free

A woman's journey back to wholeness is not an easy one. At least mine hasn't been. Sometimes we don't know where to begin, or how to take the first step toward real moments, because we have not experienced true emotional freedom in so long. Have you ever seen documentaries about animals who are brought up from birth in cages? When the cage door is finally opened, the animal almost always refuses to come out. You would think it would run from its cage, relieved to finally be free, but that is not what happens. In the animal's mind, the cage door is still there, because it has always been there. And so it sits passively in its little prison, frightened to move beyond what has become a safe habitat.

Sometimes the habit of losing ourselves is
stronger than the habit of being ourselves and
so we aren't sure how to run free.

Here is a true story about how I learned to let my spirit run free:

✦

Several years ago, I began to experience a powerful restlessness. This restlessness was no stranger to me—since I was sixteen, it had moved in and out of my life like the wind, and each time it appeared, it would stir up everything I had neatly arranged and cause trouble. Or more accurately, I would cause trouble, for when I felt the wind of restlessness begin to whirl inside of me, I would go into a kind of spiritual heat, and begin madly searching for something to appease my sudden hunger for change. When the feeling wasn't that strong, I would do things like clean out my entire house, or trade in my car for a new one, or plan an exotic trip. But there were a few times when the restlessness would overtake me so completely that I would feel swept away, and end up doing something quite dramatic like having an illicit love affair, or getting a divorce, or changing careers. This restless wind never really blew me off my course, and everything would always work out as it was meant to in the end, for I never made changes that weren't overdue anyway. But the suddenness of the process was often exhausting, painful to others, and frightening to me in its intensity.

When Jeffrey and I began our relationship, I felt like someone who has a disease they are keeping a secret. What could I say to him: "Look, this thing happens to me sometimes—I go a little crazy, and this other part of me emerges, but if you should see me go through this, remember that it's nothing personal"? I was so frightened of blowing it, of sabotaging our relationship and losing the best thing that ever happened to me. Of course, I had no intention of doing this, but then again, I never did. *"This time,"* I vowed to myself, *"when it happens, I will be ready."* And so I waited for the wind.

And it came, a delightful little breeze of everyday adrenaline at first, and then gusting into the old familiar urge to break free—but of what? This time, I was happy. This time, I knew I needed to stay right where I was. This time, I didn't need the wind to liberate me from a relationship or situation I had been stuck in.

And so day after day, I fought the forces inside of me that whispered: "Run . . . run . . ." Who was it that was calling to me, I wondered. What did they want me to run from? Where did they want me to run to? I prayed for the answers to these questions, and asked that I be shown the truth, given the wisdom to win my battle.

My Teacher, Crystal

Spiritual teachers come to us in many forms. They are not always dressed in white robes. They don't necessarily have to even know they are teachers at all. They show up in your life when you need a reminder, and point the way.

My teacher during this turbulent time was a dog named Crystal. Crystal was a beautiful Siberian husky that lived across the street from me. I had spent my whole life being scared to death of all dogs, especially large ones, until I got my own dog Bijou. He helped me make friends with all of the dogs in the neighborhood, and introduced me to the magical world of animals. So when my neighbors brought Crystal home as a little puppy, I knew it was my chance to know a big dog from the time it was small, and conquer my fear completely.

As soon as Crystal was ready for visitors, Bijou and I began going over to her yard to play. I was her first friend outside of her family, and Bijou, as it turned out, would be her first and only dog friend. She was still quite small, so even little Bijou could manage to romp with her without getting trampled, but each day she grew by leaps and bounds, and I knew it wouldn't be long before she weighed almost one hundred pounds.

One day during the summer when Crystal was just four months old, my neighbor told me they would be leaving for a few days, and Crystal would be alone except for a friend of the family who would stop in to feed her. I remember being quite concerned. "She's only a puppy," I thought to myself.

But she had already grown to be quite a big dog, and I was reassured that she would be O.K. Late that night during my sleep, I was awakened by an eerie sound. At first I wasn't sure what I was listening to—I just knew it pierced my heart. Then, I realized it was Crystal. She was howling like a wolf, crying out with loneliness.

I crept out of bed and walked in the dark to my neighbors' empty house and through the back gate. There was Crystal, sitting on the porch shaking, her thick fur shining silver in the moonlight. I ran over and hugged her. "Poor Crystal," I crooned. "Everyone left you, and you don't understand that they're coming back. Poor baby." I held her muscular body and rocked her back and forth as she nuzzled against me. When I left, I promised to return the next day to make sure she was all right.

To my surprise, we had a huge rainstorm the following morning. It rarely rains in Southern California in July, but it did that day. I realized that Crystal was unprotected. Naturally her owners didn't think it would rain, and so she had no covering over her porch. I quickly gathered up dry blankets and plastic garbage bags, and ran over to Crystal's house. She was standing there waiting for me, soaking wet and shivering. And again, I held her, made a dry place for her to lie down, and told her everything would be fine.

In a few days, her owners came back and thanked me for what I'd done, but things were never the same between Crystal and me. *We were connected now, linked together by a powerful bond I didn't quite understand.* It was more than the fact that I'd taken care of her. There was a mysterious force that joined us. I began to feel very unhappy seeing Crystal locked up behind her gates. She had a big backyard to run around in, but she was never taken out for walks, and hadn't seen the world outside her home. Each time I passed the house with Bijou, Crystal would poke her head through the fence and begin to cry. Tears would fill my eyes, and it was all I could do to not grab her and run for the hills. "I don't know what it is about that dog that moves me so much," I'd comment to Jeffrey. "I know her family loves her, and she loves them. I just keep wanting to get her out from behind the fence." I couldn't stop thinking about Crystal, and I didn't know why.

Crystal's Escape

One day, as I sat at my computer writing, I thought I heard a knock at the front door. I went downstairs, and when I pulled the door open, to my utter amazement there was Crystal, sitting politely on my porch, her tail wildly wagging. "How did you get out?" I asked in disbelief as I gave her a hug. I walked her back across the street, and my neighbor was just as surprised as I was that she had escaped. "Maybe someone left the gate open," she suggested as she put Crystal back inside. I wondered if I was imagining Crystal smiling at me as I turned to go home.

Then, Crystal started digging a hole next to the gate. I knew what she was doing. She was trying to get out so she could run free. And it worked. Every few days, I would find her at my doorstep again, a wild, joyful look in her beautiful dark eyes, her paws caked with dirt, and her now huge body rippling with excitement. My neighbors kept filling up the hole and Crystal kept digging, and repeating her escape ritual. And I silently cheered her on.

One evening before bed, I began reading *Women Who Run with the Wolves*. Clarissa Pinkola Estés writes beautifully about *La Loba*, the One Who Knows, the Wild Woman in each of us who needs to be resurrected and allowed to run free. That night, I dreamed about Crystal. I saw her furtively digging to escape her carefully fenced-in yard. I heard her calling to me with an ancient howl. And when I awoke the next morning, I understood everything:

Crystal was my mirror, the embodiment of my own Wild Woman, the passionate, mysterious, instinctual part of myself that I had kept locked behind closed doors throughout my entire life. She had been crying out to me from her comfortable yet confining prison, the cry of one who longs for the freedom to move without restriction, to run with abandon, to sing with her soul-voice. Her cry had summoned me, and without knowing why, my own restless spirit had howled back. *We were sisters, we belonged to the same pack. And she knew this before I did, for in her wise wolf way, she had looked into my eyes and seen my soul pacing back and forth, digging at the dirt under my self-erected gates, yearning to run free.*

Each time Crystal showed up at my door, I had celebrated her escapes because that is what I needed to do—to dig myself out of my own emotional fences, the shoulds and should nots by which I'd been living my life, the limits I put on which parts of me I could show my husband, my friends, my public, and which parts I had to hide. Now I understood the restlessness. Now I understood the voice that would suddenly appear in my head and whisper: "Run . . . run . . . " It was my Wild Woman, emerging from beneath the dirt where I kept trying to bury her, warning me that I would suffocate unless I broke through my own barriers. No wonder I would go wild every five years or so, and do something shocking and unconventional! I was like a chained dog who finally escapes, and tears up every trash can in the neighborhood with all of her pent-up energy.

Crystal had shown me the answer:

> It was not escape I was looking for, it was
> freedom. I didn't want to run away.
> I just wanted to run.

After each of her adventures, Crystal always obediently returned home. She didn't want to leave permanently. She just wanted to leave sometimes. And that was my truth as well. I knew I would no longer need to leave where I was to find my freedom. *I just needed to let my Wild Woman out for more runs.*

So that is how Crystal taught my spirit to run free. I do not have the storms of restlessness like I used to, just breezes. When they come, I know I am overdue for a run, and I take a day for myself, or write poetry, or spend time with women, or go to a Grateful Dead concert and dance my feet off. And then I come home.

How do you know when you need to take your spirit out for a run? *You become irritable, annoyed, bored, critical, confused, tired, or a little crazy.* You want to eat bad things, give your children away, tell your husband to find his own damn car keys, check into a hotel by yourself, order room service, and watch romantic movies all night. All this means is that your Wild Woman is calling to you. Go to her. Find out what she is really hungry for, feed her, then take her out to play.

Soon after my awakening with Crystal, her family moved back East and took her with them. Their new home is on several acres of land, and Crystal now runs wherever she pleases. I miss her very much, and think of her every time I pass that old gate, but my heart smiles to know she is happy, for her spirit has told me so. She will always be one of my most treasured teachers.

Run free, my Wolf-Sister.
The land beneath your feet rejoices to feel you dancing upon it.

Finding Real Moments for Ourselves

Here are some ways that we can create real moments for ourselves as women.

✦ Seek solitude.

Women need quiet times when the only voice we hear is our own. We are so used to making everyone else's voice more important than ours. This is a habit with most of us, especially if we grew up thinking that God is male.

> If we were taught that the doorway to God
> is through a male,
> we look outside of ourselves and our femaleness
> for spiritual connection, and not within.

For a long time, I depended upon men to give me direction and guidance, and did not trust my own inner voice. I spent most of my life setting men up as one sort of savior or another. Most of them did not object to the status I conferred upon them. I've had a guru, a husband who thought he was a guru, and business associates who wanted me to think they were my guru. I was so busy listening to their opinions that I never had time to discover my own.

Give yourself times of silence, so your voice of wisdom can emerge. It needs to become strong so it won't be shouted down by all the other voices in your life that may try to talk you out of your feelings or your knowing. Keep a journal where only your voice has a say. Take a walk in a quiet place. Listen. Soon, you will hear your own spirit talking to you.

✦ Give birth to something.

When a woman gives birth, she is tuned in to her magic, the ability to change the form of things. So anytime you want a real moment, give birth to something. It doesn't matter what you give birth to—a garden, a cake, a innovative idea at work, a bedtime story for your children, a letter to a friend, a healing for yourself, or a clean kitchen. You will feel the creative life force flowing through you, connecting you to Mother Nature herself.

I believe that we need to give birth regularly or we lose our connection to real moments. There are some women who keep getting pregnant over and over again, not because they are ready for or want another child, but because they are addicted to the process of giving birth as their only connection to their personal and spiritual power. Often, it is their own rebirth they are unconsciously seeking. They desperately need to give birth to themselves, to the lost pieces of their spirit, to their creativity.

We need to see all of our creative acts as ones of giving birth, not just those when we physically produce a child. I don't have any children of my own. But I am a mother. I have brought forth life in many forms. I have given birth to much love.

All women are mothers, because we bring forth
life and love wherever we go.

✦ *Seek the company of other women as teachers, sisters, and friends.*

Women need feminine mirrors in which to discover their own beauty. When we come together with other women, we are empowered in our wholeness. We remember who we are. We recall the steps to our Dance.

Throughout the ages, women have always had female teachers, grandmothers, and wise elders from whom they sought protection and Initiation. They guided us on our path and reminded us of our grace and dignity. But for many centuries now, we have been living in a patriarchal society. We have given men the power to define us, to teach us, to tell us our place. We have lost our connection to the Ancient Mothers from whom all life has sprung. We have forgotten our magic. We have lost our way.

Since I began my spiritual journey at age eighteen, I have had only male teachers. I honor them for all they taught me about strength and about silence. But they could not teach me about being a woman. And so for the past few years, as I have struggled to come back to wholeness, I have longed for a female teacher and guide. I prayed to find her, and I knew that until we met, I would not be complete.

Earlier this year, Jeffrey and I were in Big Sur, California, making arrangements for our wedding, which was to be several months later. One of the women helping us approached me and said, "This may sound a little strange, but I found the names of a Native American couple in the back of a book I happened to be reading this morning, and I wanted to tell you about them. They are cofounders of a nonprofit organization called 'One Earth, One People Peace Vision,' which is dedicated to restoring respectful relationships between humanity and all living things. For some reason, I thought of you and the work you do, and felt you should have their address and phone number." I thanked her, and when I took the paper from her hand, something told me I needed to call right away.

And so I did, and we arranged to meet the next day in the little historic town where they live, San Juan Bautista, one of the original California missions. Their names are Juan Jose Reyna, Jr., who everyone calls Sonny, and Elaine Reyna, who is known as Bluebird. Sonny is a writer, environmentalist, and Native American spiritual leader. Elaine is an artist/visionary and designer of traditional and contemporary ethnic clothing. When Bluebird walked up to me in their store and art gallery, and looked into my eyes, I suspected that she was the woman I had been searching for.

We sat outside in a sun-filled courtyard and began talking,

not about superficial subjects, but about who all of us really were, because we already felt a powerful connection. Jeffrey shared with them about his life, his dreams, his healing work as a chiropractor. Then I spoke about my path as a seeker, the lessons I had learned along the way, and my longing to know more.

Bluebird listened intently, and when I was finished, she looked deeply into me and said: "You know, Barbara, what you need is a Big Sister." My eyes filled with tears. I have never had a sister, not even a woman older than myself to guide me. And in that moment, I knew I had found her, and that she had found me too. "Welcome home to our indigenous family!" she proclaimed. "We are related in the spirit, and I am so happy to be reunited with you again, Little Sister."

Since that day, Bluebird has been my Big Sister, my teacher, my friend. "Women need to remember that we are sacred, that we are life givers," she reminds me. "Thank the Creator for the experience of Life, and celebrate it as the most precious treasure, the sorrow and the joy." This beautiful and humble woman is teaching me how to honor the Earth and all it produces, how to honor myself as a woman, and how to have real moments every day.

✦

My own female spiritual teachers, Crystal and Bluebird, have not come in very traditional forms, because I am not a very traditional woman, but yours do not have to be so unusual. You have many teachers waiting to guide you, many beautiful female spirits to help you on your journey back to real moments. Look around you to your grandmothers, your aunts, your friends, your daughters, and you will find them. Ask, and their presence will be revealed to you. You do not have to take the journey alone.

I dedicate this chapter to my Big Sister and
teacher, Bluebird,
whose spirit sits gently on my shoulder and
beckons me to follow her,
over the earth,
into the river,
above the sky.

"Fly, Little Sister," she whispers.
And I do. . . .

• 9 •

MEN AND REAL MOMENTS

"I have now reigned about fifty years in victory or peace, beloved by my subjects, dreaded by my enemies, and respected by my allies. Riches and honors, power and pleasure, have waited on my call, nor does any earthly blessing appear to have been wanting to my felicity. In this situation, I have diligently numbered the days of pure and genuine happiness which have fallen to my lot: They amount to fourteen."

— ASCRIBED TO ABD ER-RAHMAN III
OF SPAIN, A.D. 960

It is not easy for men to have real moments and they are suffering greatly because of it. The women who love them are suffering. Their children are suffering. The world is suffering.

I cannot write about men as a man, as I can about women. But I can tell you what I've seen as I've loved and worked with the men in my life, and what I've learned from the men who've asked me to be their teacher. These observations are careful but admitted generalizations—they may not be accurate for all men, but they do express a truth that I believe is relevant to most men.

That truth is this: that men are dying because they don't have enough real moments—they are dying emotionally because they deprive themselves of the love and intimacy they need; they are dying physically because, in their hunger for

196

accomplishment, their lives are often so out of balance that they don't know when to stop and rest, so their bodies just give out; and they are dying spiritually because they aren't sure how to turn within and begin their journey toward the sacred.

If you are a woman who loves a man, you probably already suspect this about him. Something is missing. You can't quite put your finger on it. It has nothing to do with how hard he works, or how much free time he has. It doesn't matter how old he is. It is not a material thing. Rather, it is about a place inside of him that he rarely goes to, the place of just being there, of silent, receptive feeling, of opening to the mystery of love. This is the place where you long to meet him. You arrive. You wait. He doesn't show up.

If you are a man, you may experience this hunger for real moments that I speak of in different terms, men's terms. It is a longing to take a rest from the incessant, pounding rhythm of movement that permeates your life. It is an uncomfortable yearning to go somewhere, be somewhere different from where you are, a yearning you know will not be satisfied by changing jobs, cars, or women. It is the sound of something calling to you from within that you want to answer but don't know how. It is a restlessness that never goes away.

Here is the thing about men and real moments:

> Real moments are about being, they are not
> about doing. And men are doers.

Men have been trained since the beginning of time to be good at doing—they hunted, they built, they protected. That was their role, and thus it was through their work, their toil, and their accomplishment that they defined themselves, and found their value. Women, on the other hand, were required to be good at relating—we pleased, we nurtured, we connected. We became skilled at feeling and being.

In our twentieth century, these roles have begun slowly to change, but we cannot forget that they have been in place for a long time. Habits die hard. And genetic memory influences much of our values and behavior. I always remember my mother telling me how different I was from my brother when we were babies. "You were content to sit and watch people, to color, to play with paper dolls," she'd explain. "But Michael always had to be moving. He never stopped." And she's right. We called my brother "The Furniture Mover," because even as a little boy, he was always trying to move things from one place to another. If he couldn't move the objects in our house, he would keep himself moving. We have old films of Michael, before he could even talk, running around and around in circles.

Men are movers. It's in their blood. *And so when men look for meaning, they look to their work, to what they are* doing, *whether that activity is completing a project, building new shelves for the garage, or playing a good hand of cards.* This is where they think they will find satisfaction.

But the nature of men's work has changed radically. From a conqueror, an adventurer, a soldier, men have been transformed into accountants, salesmen, and computer programmers. They are displaced warriors and unemployed explorers. Their work does not always provide them with the instant satisfaction that building a house for the family, fighting off the enemy, or plowing a field gave their great-great-great-grandfathers. It is often so removed from obvious meaning that it does not allow them to have many real moments.

✦

Men are at home in the physical world, the world of the concrete. They feel comfortable with what they can see and touch and measure. **They are goal-oriented.** That is why they put such a high value on *doing,* because it produces a result that fits into their model of what is worthwhile.

The kinds of experiences that offer you a real moment are not, as we have seen, necessarily moments of obvious achievement or accomplishment. They are quieter, subtler, and *their benefits are not so much tangible as they are invisible.* So these aren't experiences that men naturally value, because they can't easily measure how they could be meaningful. If I'm a man and I work two extra hours and get overtime pay, that's a benefit I can put in my pocket—that's meaningful. But if I spend those same two hours talking with my wife, or walking by myself, where's the benefit? **I can't measure it, and so it doesn't appear to hold as much meaning and value for me as working overtime did.**

This difference in values produces constant conflict and frustration in relationships between men and women. You mention to your husband that you'd like to spend some time just talking with him. "About what?" he responds. Suddenly, you feel annoyed, confused. Why do you have to give him an agenda of what you'd like to discuss? Isn't it enough that he knows you want to talk? No, it is not. Just talking together and sharing intimate time probably does not hold the same value for him as a man, who places a great deal of importance on doing, as it does for you as a woman, who places a great deal of importance on relating and being.

Women, when we stop taking care of everyone else and get around to focusing on ourselves, are good at just being. That is why we crave nondoing experiences, especially with our partners. We know they will produce delicious real moments.

Men need to find nondoing experiences as
meaningful experiences.

Men need to stop looking for the instant benefit they will receive from an experience, and feel what is actually going on in the moment, right here and right now. *Real moments are in the realm of the timeless and the invisible. Their value cannot be calculated or measured.* If you try to measure it, you aren't having a real moment anymore.

✦

"To be on a quest is nothing more or less than to become an asker of questions."

— SAM KEEN

The journey back to real moments is a journey characterized by questions, as we talked about in Chapter Four— questions like "Who am I?" "Am I living the life I want to lead, or the life others want me to lead?" "Am I happy?" "Do I give enough love? Do I get enough love?" In order to ask questions, you have to conquer the fear of not knowing, and discover the courage to live with uncertainty for a while.

This is not an easy task for men. Men are of the earth. They need the solid, the certain, the well-marked path. *They are often uncomfortable with, even frightened of, the unformed, the vague, the fluctuating, the mysterious* . . . (and of course that is a good description of the female psyche!). This can make it difficult for them to question, to search, to explore the un-known—it is unfamiliar territory.

Women like asking questions.
Men like having answers.

To ask a question implies that one doesn't know the an-swer. Women, as a rule, are not afraid of "I don't know," which is a form of intellectual free-fall. After all, we are good at surrender and letting go. We practice this every time we make love, menstruate, give birth, and kiss our children good-bye as we send them off to school. You will find more women involved in personal growth, belonging to support groups, buying self-help books and seeking therapy because we are comfortable, even stimulated by asking questions, and we aren't usually in a hurry to get to the answers.

Men, however, *like to know. To men knowing is a form of doing, a show of mental strength.* I have seen men go to great lengths to avoid saying the words "I don't know." Instead, they utter statements such as *"I don't want to talk about it," "Why aren't you ever satisfied?" "Don't you ever shut up?"* or *"Just relax, everything is under control."* They do not want to admit that they do not have the answer clear in their minds just yet, so they stall, avoid responding, or, if you are insistent, try scaring you off with anger in order to find the time to figure things out and get to a place of knowing and certainty.

Being unwilling not to know hurts men.
It keeps them stuck where they are.

It prevents them from moving forward, from
breaking through to new levels of emotional and
spiritual freedom.

In his important book *Fire in the Belly,* Sam Keen describes a man's sacred quest for himself as a journey of passages . . . *"from cocksureness to potent doubt . . . from having the answers to living the questions."* Living the questions means living in a constant state of surrender and loss of control. This is the antithesis of what men have been trained to do. Instead, they have been taught to dominate, conquer, hold out, prevail, and not give in. I say this with tremendous respect. It is these same qualities that have enabled a man to fight off his enemy, kill to protect his land and family, venture into dark forests to hunt for food so those he loves can survive, stand with his brothers against the oppressors who want to take away his freedom, climb up one more mountain in order to find a safe spot for his new home.

But in his quest for real moments, a man has to muster up the courage to turn his back on the ways of the warrior, for they are destroying him and his relationships. It means learning to say to your lover: *"I'm not sure," "I need time to think about it," "Could you slow down? I'm not sure what you mean," "What do you need that I'm not giving you?" "How can we do it differently?" and "I'm sorry."* It means being willing, at times, to live with uncertainty, to open to the mysterious and unexpected, to enter into a moment with no agenda other than to fully experience it, and to know through it all that you are still a man.

That is all we, as women, want from you. **We want you to take the journey with us.** We want to explore together. We want to be spiritual comrades. We want to discover new territories of intimacy, new realms of physical passion, and new levels of happiness. We want ascend together in love. We don't want to leave you behind.

And in spite of all of your conditioning and every cell in your body that screams: *"But if I let go, I won't be a man,"* know that, in our eyes at least, **you will be our most honored champion and our most brave hero.**

Frozen Feelings and Sacred Tears

Now, the part you men have been dreading, where I talk about feelings. You knew it was coming, didn't you? Of course. Because, in order to have real moments, whether with your lover, your children, or yourself, you have to be willing to fully feel. And that is difficult for most men to do.

For centuries, men have lived as strangers to the emotional

world where we as women thrive. **You had to become an expert at** *not* **feeling in order to survive.** How could you strangle a man with your bare hands if you were feeling compassion? How could you hold up your spear and face a wild animal charging at you full speed if you were feeling fear? How could you follow orders to throw a grenade into an enemy village, knowing innocent people would be killed if you did, but that you would be killed if you didn't, and allow yourself to feel anguish?

It is no different in the twentieth century. The modern business world can be just as vicious and demoralizing as any battlefield. Men are rewarded if they are tough and ruthless and diminished if they are perceived as "too soft." If you show fear, you are not respected. If you demonstrate unshakable confidence, you are called a leader. The weapons have changed, but the rules of the game are the same.

This is the price you paid for your manhood: *What has been required of you to "be a man" has also required you to numb yourself to feeling.* And herein lies your dilemma. You cannot kill your ability to feel terror, shame, and grief without killing your ability to feel joy, love, and compassion. And so many men walk around in a state of secret despair, their hearts full of frozen feelings that they will not or cannot release. Your woman, your children reach out to you, begging you to join us in the dance of emotion, and you shake your head "No!" We turn away and weep, concluding that you do not love us, never guessing your carefully hidden secret: You have forgotten the steps.

If you are honest with yourself, if you turn your attention inward, you will feel the psychic scars you inherited along with your manhood, those ancient wounded places that keep you from living as joyfully as you deserve to, that keep you from dancing with wild abandon alongside of those you love, that keep you from having real moments. **These scars, these** wounds must be your new landscape to conquer if you wish to live authentically and fully as a human being and a man. Sam Keen again says it in a male voice: "*Men have much to mourn before they can be reborn.*"

To conquer a wound, you must heal it, and to heal it, you must feel it.

Facing your wounds, and melting your frozen feelings requires courage, forgiveness, and tears. *I believe that all tears are sacred, that they let us know the ice around our heart is melting.* Tears are not easy for men, but they will give you back pieces of yourself you didn't even know you had lost. I am proud to have been present, throughout my many years of teaching, when thousands of men have cried again for the first time since they were little boys. These are sacred occasions, just as birth is sacred—a new being is emerging into the world. It helps to have an understanding, caring midwife there to catch you when you break through your veneer of numbness—any open, loving woman will do, preferably your own!

Some of *women's* most treasured real moments with the men we love occur when you give us the gift of sharing your tears.

When Jeffrey trusts me enough to show me his pain, and allows me to hold him and comfort him while he navigates through it, I am overwhelmed with gratitude. He has opened the door to the inner sanctum of his heart, and invited me in. There is no greater intimacy.

Do the emotional work you know you need to do. This is the most important commitment you can make to your marriage, to your children, or to yourself.

The Curse of the Pack: Male Loneliness

Men like being part of a pack. They like watching sporting events in packs, drinking in packs, talking around the water cooler in packs, going on a fishing trip in packs. In the pack, they feel safe. In the pack, they get to not feel alone, without being pressured to reveal anything of themselves. **In spite of this, most men I know are lonely, not because they lack companionship, but because of their inability to experience real moments together.**

This is not an obvious loneliness—it is more like a deep sense of isolation. Men share the unimportant things, like who won last night's game, how much they paid for a new muffler, and what they think of the new secretary's legs. But they keep their dreams and secrets carefully hidden from each other. It is not uncommon for "best" buddies to not even know that their friend is unhappy in his marriage, worried about an aging parent, has a sexual problem, or is months behind on paying his bills. They just don't talk about this stuff.

A recent McGill report on male intimacy found the following:

- ✦ Only one out of ten men has a male friend with whom he discusses work, money, or his relationship.
- ✦ Only one out of more than twenty men has a male friend with whom he discusses his feelings about himself, sex, and other more intimate topics.

What this means is that most men never talk about anything truly important or personal with other men in their life. They never experience real moments with someone of their own sex, with their brothers in spirit.

Last month, Jeffrey and I were discussing one of our

friends, who happens to be one of Jeffrey's best friends. "It's too bad that he and his wife are going through so much right now," I commented.

"What are you talking about?" Jeffrey asked with a puzzled look on his face.

"You know, how much they have been fighting about money, and not getting along very well." I realized as I went on that Jeffrey had no idea what I was referring to. "Honey, hasn't he even mentioned this to you?"

"No," he replied in a surprised voice. "I just talked to him yesterday, and he said everything was fine. When did you talk to him?"

"Today, and he broke down and cried on the phone with me."

We both shook our heads in amazement, realizing that Jeffrey didn't even know what was going on in the personal life of such a close friend. So what was my secret for getting him to open up? It was simple . . . I asked him how his marriage was doing, and when I heard the hesitation in his voice, I reached out and invited him to talk about it, something most men would feel too uncomfortable to do. I violated the male taboo that says "Don't get too personal," but because I am a woman, I got away with it.

✦

There is a certain comfort level men exhibit when they are in a group that disappears the moment they are alone with just one other man. That is because the dynamic between two people demands intimacy, and if you think intimacy with a woman is frightening to a man, you can begin to imagine the secret panic he feels when faced with the prospect of being intimate with another man.

If you are a man, imagine for a moment that it's late at night, and you are sitting by a fire talking with another man.

You are sharing your deepest feelings, your most private thoughts, and he is doing the same. You feel understood in a way you haven't for a long time, a way that even the woman you love can never understand you, for she is not a man. The connection between you and your friend feels alive and powerful. There is a tangible force flowing between you, of brotherhood, of sameness.

Suddenly, you become uncomfortable. You are experiencing love with another man. If you are heterosexual, you panic, thinking "I shouldn't be feeling this way. What does this mean?" and you will do something in that moment to sever the intensity of the connection—make a joke, get up and stretch, change the subject. Perhaps you will even avoid the person afterward, going out of your way to diminish any importance the experience might have had for you. I've known some men to actually create an artificial reason for ending the friendship because they became so frightened at feeling love for another man.

This is all fear-based, homophobic behavior. *It is a total misinterpretation of a powerful moment of love for sexual attraction.* You make the mistake of trying to give the experience significance and consequences beyond what it is—**a real moment of love.** Most men don't even let themselves get this far in sharing intimacy with one another. In unconscious anticipation and avoidance of such a horrifying experience, they keep all men at arm's length. And in the process, they end up with no truly intimate friends of their own sex.

The fear most men have of experiencing
intimacy with one another makes male
friendship awkward.

I'm not letting women totally off the hook here. We, too, have our tolerance level for feelings of love with a girlfriend before we get uncomfortable, but it's way past where most men would have already run out the door screaming.

✦

"Having no soul union with other men can be the most damaging wound of all."

— ROBERT BLY

Every man needs to bond with other men from the heart. He needs replacements for the kind of brothers and fathers he always wanted and perhaps never had. He need to fulfill his needs for intimacy with someone other than his lover, so she isn't his only outlet for feeling (which will eventually drive her crazy and make him resentful). He need mirrors of his own quest to understand his masculinity, soul buddies who can validate his journey like no woman ever can.

Find a friend. Take off your mask. Show him who you really are. Don't be afraid of how close you feel . . . it's just love.

✦

A word to men who love women: This is what your lover wishes she could say to you:

"Do you want to know the secret for making me truly happy? Share real moments with me. That is what I am hungry for. That is what I have been trying to tell you. The sudden embrace after dinner, the kiss in the bathroom for no reason at all, the call from work just to say 'I love you,' the moment during lovemaking when you hug me tight as if to say 'Yes, I am here with you, right now, the only place in the world I wish to be'—this is what I need.

"When I seem angry or melancholy or anxious, it is not because I need a vacation, or because my hormones are acting up—it is because I cannot find you. I'm reaching out to you through the darkness, but your hand does not reach back to

grasp mine. I'm calling to you in my heart, but my plea is greeted only by your silence. Where have you gone? I miss you, not your body, or your conversation, but your precious spirit.

"This is what I want from you—to meet me at the place where love resonates in your heart. For just one moment, feel how much you love me, feel it until you want to burst, and right then, gently take my face in your hands, look into my eyes, and drown me with your love."

✦

"If you observe a really happy man you will find him building a boat, writing a symphony, educating his son, growing double dahlias in his garden, or looking for dinosaur eggs in the Gobi desert. He will not be searching for happiness as if it were a collar button that has rolled under the radiator. He will not be striving for it as a goal in itself. He will have become aware that he is happy in the course of living life twenty-four crowded hours of the day."

— W. BERAN WOLFE

Some final tips before you begin your journey toward more real moments:

. . . Take regular quiet time away from everyone
where you can be alone with yourself.
. . . Start a journal. It may seem corny, but
women have known the secret power of writing
down their thoughts for centuries. No one needs
to read it but you.
. . . Cultivate a special buddy you can grow with.
. . . Do less.
. . . Question more.
. . . Walk the land.
. . . Listen to your heart.

. . . And when in doubt, ask the woman in your life to help you practice having more real moments.

. . . It will be our pleasure . . .

· 10 ·

REAL MOMENTS
AND THE FAMILY

"Fifty years from now,
it will not matter what kind of car you drove,
what kind of house you lived in,
how much you had in your bank account
nor what your clothes looked like.
But the world will be a little better
because you were important in the life of a child."
— ANONYMOUS

Everything I have written so far in this book about experiencing real moments can be applied to your relationship with your family—your parents, your children, your brothers and sisters, and your chosen family of friends. This chapter contains some additional thoughts about families with children, because there are special and important things we need to remember about loving our children, and because in these challenging and often frightening times, our children need our love and support more than ever before.

◆

Children are powerful seeds that grow up into gardens. What we plant into the mind and heart of one child will one day affect thousands of people. That is why children have always been associated with hope—they are our opportunity to break free from the cycle, to throw off the chains of the past and make the future better. They are a doorway into healing and new beginnings.

What your children become will ultimately reflect back on you. You will always be one of the most powerful influences in their lives, because it was your job to nurture the seed so it could become the garden. Instinctively, you know this, and so you try to give your children all the things you never had, and to take care of them in every way possible. But in your sincere efforts, you may have forgotten one crucial truth:

> You cannot be a good parent if you don't take care of yourself.

If your job is to water the seed-souls of your children, you need to make sure *your* watering can is full. You need to keep your own heart filled up. You need to make sure you are giving yourself enough love, support, and real moments first before you can give to your kids.

Filling ourselves up first is something many parents fail at miserably, in the name of forfeiting our needs for the needs of our children. The baby-boomers of the fifties and sixties are particularly guilty of this pattern. We have attempted to become superparents, to offer our children all of the recreational activities, educational opportunities, and material possessions our parents couldn't give us. True, there are many neglectful parents out there as well, who use the television as an electronic baby-sitter, and don't even notice when their own children are attention starved. *But the majority of us feel guilty when we take time for ourselves,* fearful that one day when they are grown up, our children will point at us accusingly, saying "It's all your fault—if you hadn't taken that vacation [gone to the gym, spent that afternoon with your friend, gone back to school], I wouldn't be the mess I am today!"

I know a woman who lives for her children. She has given up every hobby, interest, even her friends, if it means taking any time away from her two girls. Recently, I convinced her to meet me for lunch, not an easy task. I stopped to pick her up, and from the good-bye scene at her house, you would have thought she was leaving for a three-week trip to Africa— she went over five lists with the baby-sitter, told the kids over and over again that she would only be gone for two hours, and apologized for even leaving at all. No sooner had we arrived at the restaurant than she called home to see how the children were doing.

"Marlene," I said, "it's only been twenty minutes since you left. Do you really need to call them now?"

"Well, they aren't used to me being gone," she responded, shaking her head. "They get upset when I'm not around."

"But they aren't little babies anymore," I reminded her. "They're five and seven years old. How will they ever learn to be independent?"

"Maybe I do go overboard a little bit, but I don't want them to ever feel neglected like I did when I was a child."

This was not an easy conversation for me to have with my friend. How could I tell her how much she had been neglecting herself? How could I let her know how insecure I saw her children becoming, because they hadn't learned to let go of her, even a little bit?

✦

"Nothing has a stronger influence psychologically on their environment, and especially on their children, than the unlived life of the parents."

— C. G. JUNG

When you neglect yourself for the sake of your sons and daughters, you are not doing them any favors. *If you are living for or through your children, and ignoring your own needs, all you are teaching them is how to sacrifice who they are in order to make someone else happy,* a value which never works in the end. Perhaps when they are still very young, they will love being waited on hand and foot. But this will render them spoiled and unimaginative, and when they're older, they will look at you and see an unhappy figure with unfulfilled dreams. And they will feel guilty that you threw all of that away for their sake.

I can promise you one thing: Your kids will never grow up and say *"Mom, Dad, I am so grateful that you totally sacrificed your own happiness, intimate relationship, and growth as a human being so I would never hear the word 'No.' I'm glad you were miserable so that I could have everything I wanted. Thank you for not fully living your lives. I plan to follow in your footsteps and give up all the fun and personal satisfaction in my life when I have children."*

Children learn from watching you live.
If you take the time to have real moments for
yourself, they will learn to do the same for
themselves.

If you take the time to feed your own heart, your children will learn to feed theirs, and not to run on emotional empty. *Instead of sacrificing your life for your children, live your life as a model for them to emulate.*

✦

"The best thing to spend on your children is your time."
—LOUISE HART

What do children really want from us, the grown-ups in their lives?

✦ They want to feel loved and valued.
✦ They want to feel like they make a difference in our lives.
✦ They want to feel they are O.K. just the way they are.
✦ They want to feel like we are proud of them, and don't wish they had been born to someone else.

Every child needs to know his or her parents feel this way in order to develop a healthy level of self-esteem and self-love.

> Sharing real moments with your child is the
> best way to show him how important he is to
> you and to give him a powerful experience
> of feeling your love

Love, not toys, makes children feel worthwhile. Unfortunately in our society we shower our children with material possessions in an attempt to make up for the real moments of connection we are lacking. For many parents, it is easier, less time consuming, and less confrontational to buy their child a new toy than to share some honest, loving moments together.

One of the most amazing stories I heard in the days following the Los Angeles earthquake had to do with this very same confusion of values. The earthquake hit at 4:31 A.M. on a Monday. A few hours later, a television reporter was out with a camera investigating the damage, when he saw an enormous line of people winding around a building. He assumed that these people were lining up to receive emergency aid, water rations, or to buy flashlights, since most of the city was without power. But this was not the case.

Why were thousands of people standing in line only hours after a major disaster? They were anticipating a new delivery of Power Rangers, the "hot" toy of the moment, to a local toy store!!! These parents had left their frightened children at home with friends or relatives amidst the broken glass and during repeated aftershocks, to wait for three hours until the store opened so they could buy plastic warrior midgets!

I'm sure those parents had good intentions. Certainly, many of them were thinking *"I'll bet this Power Ranger will make little Jimmy feel better."* But plastic fighting men were not what the terrified children in Los Angeles really needed that morning. They needed to know they would be safe if an earthquake of that size or greater happened again. They needed to talk about their terror; they needed to be held; **they needed love.**

> When you give your children material things
> as replacements for love,
> you teach them that it is objects, not love,
> which will bring them happiness.

It is a tragedy that so many children end up with lots of things but have few real moments of intimacy with their parents. Intimacy isn't a word we usually associate with children—we use it to describe the experience of closeness we have with a lover. The word "intimacy" comes from the Latin, *intimus*, which means innermost. So really, **intimacy is the experience of connecting with the innermost part of another person. Experiencing intimacy with your children happens when your souls touch—and that is the most lovely of real moments.**

Your children crave these real moments with you. They want intimacy. They want your time and your complete attention. When you pay full attention to a child, he feels important, as if who he is and what he has to say has value. Ten minutes spent giving a child your undivided attention and love is worth ten hours of dragging him around from one attraction to another, but not really paying any attention to the person inside of him at all.

How many of us, now that we are adults, love our parents, but feel they do not really know us? How many of us feel they never took the time to understand the person we are inside, with all of our hopes and all of our fears? How many of us who were given "things" look back in vain for a memory, any memory, of a moment of true connection and unconditional love? *How many of us still weep because our mother or father doesn't get who we really are?*

Sit down with your child. Look deeply into his heart. Listen carefully to his words. Discover the unique and beautiful spirit he is inside. There is no one else like him in the world.

Children are on loan from God. Pay attention
to who has been sent to you for caretaking.

Guilty Love: *The Dilemma of Being a Divorced Parent*

Bringing up children is always challenging, but it is even more so for single and divorced parents. They often feel consumed by the guilt of the failed relationship, and terribly frightened that this failure puts their children at risk for developing emotional problems down the line. **So they become good at what I call "guilty love," a smothering, selfless, nonstop kind of attention they focus on their kids.** It's as if they sentence themselves to a form of penance: *"I've ruined my children's lives by getting divorced, so now I can't have any more fun. I won't date, I won't see my friends, and maybe that will begin to make up for my sins."* These parents find it even harder to take the time for their own personal real moments, or to have them with their children.

You know you are a victim of guilty love when, as a parent, you feel almost ashamed and defensive doing something just for you. You find yourself constantly apologizing to your children for things you shouldn't have to make excuses about:

"Mommy has to go out to the dentist for a few hours today, but I promise for the rest of the week we'll be together every second, O.K.?" The message this gives a child is that you exist for the sole purpose of being their slave, and that anytime you fulfill a personal need, you are breaking the rules.

I have a friend who is a divorced father. He refuses to get into a new relationship because it "might not be good for the kids." When his children visit for the weekend, he won't even take phone calls from friends. "I don't want them to feel abandoned by me again," he explains. Can you imagine what his children are like? They are self-absorbed, selfish, whining little people with no sensitivity to anyone's feelings but their own. They demand constant attention and entertainment. They don't know how to be quiet or alone for five minutes. And why shouldn't they be this way? This is what their father has unintentionally taught them by always giving up his needs and desires for theirs.

Our high divorce rate has bred a whole race of *"Disneyland Dads,"* weekend fathers like my friend who attempt to fit two weeks of loving and recreation into the two days they have with their children once or twice a month. They arrive at the house armed with bribes in the form of toys and gifts that say "I brought you this so you won't be mad at me for not living with you anymore." They indulge their kids with all the junk food, scary movies, and late nights that Mom refuses to let them have. They become smiling sugar daddies, leaving all the hard work and discipline to her.

Let me tell you something as someone who was one of those children many years ago—we secretly hate those guilt gifts, those frantic visits that are supposed to make up for the fact that you aren't there to tuck us in at night, that you made Mommy cry, that our family is forever broken. We hate that proud look in your eyes when you thrust those games and dolls and dresses upon us, waiting for us to make a big deal over this latest offering, as if you really think we're too little to know we're being bought. And we feel contempt for you when, at the end of the day, you sigh with relief after feeding and entertaining us like a favorite pet, so satisfied with yourself that you were a good dad, and that everything's O.K.

And as you walk to the car and wave good-bye, we want to scream at the top of our tiny lungs: "IT'S NOT O.K.!! THOSE STUPID TOYS AND TREATS DON'T MAKE IT O.K.! WHY DON'T YOU REALLY TALK TO ME? WHY DON'T YOU NOTICE HOW MISERABLE I AM? WHY DON'T YOU JUST HOLD ME AND TELL ME HOW MUCH YOU LOVE ME?"

This is what your children want you to know, whether they are five or fifty with children of their own, whether you as their parents divorced or stayed together: **All we have ever wanted, and all we want now, is real moments with you, when you see us, accept us, and love us. That's all.**

◆

"The year my son Kevin was eight, one of our car-pool drivers was often delayed picking the kids up from school. One afternoon, when Kevin was dropped off at home particularly late, I asked him what had happened. He said that school personnel had told him to wait for his ride in the room next to the principal's office. Hadn't he been awfully bored for that half hour? 'No,' he said, 'I kept busy finding the pictures in the wallpaper.' "

— SUSAN K. PERRY
Playing Smart

Children naturally know how to have real moments. They live in the timelessness of the present. They see the everyday world as full of wonder and mystery, and with this perception, they infuse the most ordinary things with magic. The abstract designs on the wallpaper become fascinating pictures. The old scarf becomes a ball gown. The family dog becomes a fierce lion protecting the young prince. Every object, every act, takes on significance and meaning.

My fondest memories of childhood play have nothing to do with store-bought toys, but of magical moments my brother and I created together. One of our favorite things to do was to build a cave of large red cardboard blocks, take an old chiffon paisley scarf of my mother's and hang it over the entrance, and then sit in the cave for hours. We would pretend we were in an exotic Arabian tent in the desert, and with the basement light filtering through the sheer purple scarf, the inside of our hideaway was filled with a luminous glow. This was our special place to share our secrets, our fears and tell stories of how we wanted our lives to turn out.

> All children know how to open the door to the
> kingdom of wonder.

If you need to experience more real moments in your life, ask a child to take you on a tour of his or her world. Follow in their footsteps for a few hours, or a day, do whatever they are doing, play at whatever they are playing and you will remember how to see the world through a child's eyes. If you pay close attention, you will notice that children are constantly inviting you to enter their magical world, but you're refusing the invitation. **They are offering you a precious gift—the opportunity to have some real moments.**

Last week while I was taking my morning walk, I passed by a little friend of mine who lives down the street. Her name is Alex, and when I stopped to say hello, she told me she was collecting old flowers to dry and make into pictures. My first instinct was to finish my walk and rush back to my computer, since I was in the middle of writing an intense section of the book. Then I remembered that my book was entitled *Real Moments,* and that I needed to have more of them. So I asked Alex if I could help her find flowers for her collection, and suggested we look in the big garden behind my house for suitable candidates.

For the next hour, Alex and I wandered around my backyard, looking for flowers with broken stems, blossoms that were about to fall off, and petals that already lay on the ground. She showed me how different colors would look beautiful together, and how mixing twigs and leaves with the flowers would make a nice effect. After about ten minutes, I noticed that the tension I'd been feeling all day was beginning to dissipate, and soon I was feeling very centered and joyful as I collected dying flowers with my nine-year-old friend. It was a lovely afternoon.

Every few weeks, I make a point to share real moments like this with the kids in my neighborhood. Bijou and I will sit on the curb with two or three children and I'll just talk to them—about school, about their friends, about what they think and feel. They allow me to enter their world, and remind me how to make everything meaningful: we lie on our backs and notice how the clouds change shape, and see what forms they're showing us; we watch the dogs and cats play together and imagine what they are saying to one another; we talk about our favorite foods and movies. *I often feel that the time I spend on the street enjoying real moments with my small friends is probably more important for my well-being than all the books I could ever read or seminars I could ever take.*

If you have children, then you have built-in opportunities for real moments right at home. If, like me, you don't have kids of your own, borrow someone else's for a half hour, and allow them to be your guide on the road back to innocence and wonder.

You have as much to learn from children
as you have to teach them.

✦

"If you're happy, you can always learn to dance."
— OLD BALINESE SAYING

Imagine that your child is drawing abstract pictures on white paper and cutting them up into pieces. You approach and ask him what he is doing. He looks at you with annoyance — isn't it obvious what he is doing? He's drawing pictures and cutting them into pieces. What you really mean by your question is: *What is the purpose of what you're doing? What is the goal of your activity? What do you hope to accomplish?* **You are imposing your goal-oriented values on your child, thus taking him out of the moment.**

We ask children the wrong questions all the time:

"What is that for?"
"What are you going to do with that?"
"Why are you doing that?'

If we could remember back to our childhood, if we were having more real moments, we wouldn't have to ask the questions, because we would already know the answers: **"I'm just doing what I'm doing. I'm being where I am. Maybe in a moment, I'll decide to do something different with this, but right now, I'm perfectly happy doing things exactly as I am."**

It is good to teach children the importance of setting goals for themselves. But in our attempt to help them become "successful," we often rob them of their natural knowing and intuitive values, and interfere with the real moments they spontaneously create for themselves.

By always asking our children to explain the purpose of everything they do, we are teaching them that their value is in *doing*, not in *being*.

Many of our problems as adults stem from our distorted system of values that emphasizes what we accomplish, rather than who we are, as a measure of self-worth. We need to support children to break this cycle, and remind them that it is *who they are as a person, and not what they achieve, that makes them special.* Unfortunately, we cannot rely on our present educational system, which is purely goal-oriented, to teach this to our kids. **It is up to us to tell our sons and daughters, through our words and our behavior, that we love and admire them not because of what they do or do not achieve, but for the pure goodness we see shining from their hearts.**

Stop worrying about what your children will become. Stop trying to develop them into something. Your job is to help them be happy, and as the Balinese saying goes, if they are happy, they can always learn to dance, or be a doctor or an artist or whatever they want to be, because they will have mastered the most important job in life first.

Creating Real Moments with and for Your Children

Here are some other suggestions for experiencing more real moments with your children:

✦ Allow them to fully feel their emotions.

Children intuitively know that the way to release an uncomfortable emotion is to fully feel it first. They cry and wail, and five minutes later they are smiling. They have a tantrum, and in a half hour, they have forgotten what they are angry about. It is we adults who mistakenly try to get our kids to suppress their emotions by telling them "You shouldn't be upset," "That's a silly thing to cry about," "Why are you laughing so hard?" or "You have no reason to be angry." *By doing this, we pull them out of the moments in which they are being with their pain, or their joy.*

Let your children feel their feelings. Help them find words

for the emotions bubbling inside of them. Show them you understand what they are going through, and ask if there is anything you can do to help. Often, there isn't, and you need to let them be, realizing you are more upset by their pain than they are. Of course, it will help if you practice these same guidelines in your own life!

✦ Encourage your children to keep diaries or journals.

When we write down our thoughts and feelings about a day or an event, we get to step back, look at them clearly, and learn from what we see. Keeping a diary or journal is a marvelous way to create real moments for yourself as an adult, and it works just as well for children. The diary becomes a special and secret friend, an outlet for their emotions, and an opportunity to practice being mindful and paying attention to what's going on in their world. If your children are too young to write, you can have them dictate their thoughts or feelings to you, and perhaps draw pictures to go with the words. And as they grow older, they will be able to use their writing time as a form of meditation and personal exploration.

✦ Create family rituals for experiencing real moments together.

The same Love Processes I described at the end of the chapter "Real Moments and Loving" are wonderful to practice within a family. I have taught thousands of parents the *Appreciation, Gratitude,* and *Forgiveness Exercises* and heard how fulfilling it was for them to share these with their children. Some people like to set aside some time once a week, perhaps on a Sunday evening, when they sit in a circle as a family and do a Gratitude and/or Appreciation Process. Join hands, and take turns sharing "Something I'm grateful for," or "Something I really love about you," etc. Other families like to incorporate shorter versions of these exercises at the dinner table just before eating once or twice a week. And whenever there has been any upset or tension in the family, a Forgiveness Exercise is a must. Don't forget—these are not just for the children, but must include the adults as well.

In the next and final section of this book, I'll be sharing many ideas for creating real moments in your life. I encourage you to teach all of these to your children, and to make loving rituals an integral part of your family tradition.

✦

"Children are . . . very ancient souls in tiny bodies."
— MASTER ADALFO

Your children are not your children. They are your teachers, your guides, your challengers, your lesson-bringers, your truth-tellers, your heart-healers, your spirit-polishers. They are connected to a source of wisdom and love that most of us have lost in the process of growing older. They see angels, they practice unconditional love, they have cosmic connections.

All children are little mystics. They travel easily between the visible and invisible worlds. They have not yet gotten caught up in the boundaries of time and space. They know how to fly.

Until we inhibit them with our ideas of what is real and unreal, all children possess a natural spirituality. They *remember things we have forgotten, and sadly, when we don't respect and acknowledge their natural knowing, we force them to forget as well.*

There's a beautiful story I heard some time ago about a mother who'd just had her second child, another little boy. It seems that one night, as she approached the baby's room, she saw her first son, who was three, standing next to his little brother's crib, staring at the tiny figure lying there. Not wanting to disturb whatever was happening, she remained outside by the door. Then, she saw her older son lean toward his newborn brother, and in a conspiratorial tone whisper: **"Psssst. Hey . . . Jimmy. It's me . . . your brother Danny. Tell me what God looks like . . . I'm starting to forget."**

The mother's eyes filled with tears as she witnessed this sacred and real moment. She realized that Danny knew little Jimmy had just come from the world of spirit, a world Danny vaguely remembered, but was losing touch with as he identified more with his physical body and his role as a male human being called Danny. In this secret conversation, he was reaching out to Jimmy in hopes of recapturing some of the truth he could feel slipping away more and more every day.

I love this story. It says everything there is to say about who our children really are:

Welcome them into your life as your teachers
and your blessings. . . .
Allow them to show you how to find meaning
and celebration in every moment. . . .
And if you, too, have forgotten what God looks
like, ask a child to help you remember. . . .

Part Four

THE PATH TO REAL MOMENTS

Tools for Creating More Love and Meaning in Your Life

◆

· 11 ·

EVERYDAY SPIRITUALITY: Real Moments with Yourself

"The distinction between human and spiritual is made only by human beings. They are not separate. They are woven together. If you do not open your heart to human beings, you will find it difficult to open your heart to God. If you do not love human beings, including yourself, you will find it difficult to love God. Your spiritual path begins in your humanness . . ."

— RON SCOLASTICO AND THE GUIDES

Once, long ago, the peoples of the Earth knew the truth of Oneness: that matter is just the joyful song of spirit; that the human is just a playful dance of the Divine; that the Earth, the animals, the wind, the sun, and the stars are all brothers and sisters sharing one heart that beats in a cosmic rhythm. And their knowledge of Oneness blessed the days of their lives, for it made everything they experienced sacred.

But over time, the truth was forgotten, and The Way of Separation was born. And the people came to believe that God was different and outside of them, and that Nature was a word for inanimate objects like mountains and rivers and trees here to be man's servants. And they decided that some people, like priests and sages, and some places, like churches and temples, were infused with more spirit than others, and therefore were better. They placed heaven above them, and no longer saw earth as a sacred place. *Thus their everyday lives became ordinary, for they had lost their connection to the Divine.*

✦

We are the great-great-grandsons and -granddaughters of those who followed The Way of Separation. **We have separated the spiritual from everyday living, and thus separated ourselves from experiencing everyday spirituality.** The spiritual has become associated with Sunday church services, or the Sabbath, or yoga and meditation, or a trip to India, or a tour of a famous European cathedral. We think praying is more spiritual than riding a bicycle, reading religious literature more holy than making love. We are living secularized lives and yet wondering why life often feels so meaningless and devoid of purpose.

We have even separated from our very home, the Earth. We have disconnected from its rhythms. We try to tame them with technology as if the planet itself were a wild animal we are determined to dominate. We treat the Earth with hostility. If a mountain is in our way, we move it. If a tree blocks our view, we cut it down. We poison the waters and pollute the air, and *because we foolishly think of ourselves as distinct and separate, we do not see that by hurting our Mother, the Earth, we are hurting ourselves.*

The search for real moments and everyday spirituality must begin with a return to The Way of Oneness.

Everyday spirituality is not an escape from your
usual life in search of some special, exalted
experience, but a surrender into the fullness of
every experience.

It is not a path that leads you away from the human to the spiritual, from the Earth to Heaven, but rather one that leads you back into the ordinary and everyday, and invites you to find the spiritual within it. It begins and ends where you already are, right here, right now. There's nothing else to look for, nothing else to acquire. You already have everything you need.

✦

"We are not human beings having a spiritual experience. We are spiritual beings having a human experience."

— RAM DASS

When I became a seeker, I began what I called a "spiritual path." In my longing to know God, I turned away from worldly things. I practiced meditation for hours, sometimes days at a time. I spent whole years in retreat and silence, living in the mountains, seeing only other meditators. I viewed my physical body as an obstacle to enlightenment, my human desires as impediments to achieving a pure, spiritual state. And I looked at my life on Earth as some sort of prison sentence I was serving that kept me from going back "home" to my Divine origins.

I had many beautiful and uplifting experiences during those years, but I could only be happy when I was doing my "spiritual practice." After searching and searching for answers to my dilemma, I finally had the important realization that *all of human life was a spiritual practice—I was supposed to be practicing being human!!* And thus far, I hadn't been doing a very good job. In fact, I'd attempted to avoid being human entirely. No wonder I was so miserable: I was in the water, but trying not to get wet!

Since that time, I have worked on embracing my humanness, not running from it, and looking within it for the very same spiritual experiences I used to seek elsewhere. I know now that my presence here on Earth is not a sentence—it is a gift; **that being human is not a loss of spirit, but an opportu-**

nity for spirit to enjoy itself on the physical plane. I am here because I am loved.

In order to experience everyday spirituality, we need to remember that we are spiritual beings spending some time in a human body. We are not separate from spirit. This would be impossible. We are simply spirit disguised in human form. *In this way, we are connected to all life.* The flower is spirit disguised as a flower. The tomato is spirit disguised as a tomato. The rock is spirit disguised as a rock. This book you are holding is spirit disguised as a book. We all share the same source. We are all made of the same invisible particles of matter. We are all One.

As parts of the whole organism called Life, we are utterly dependent upon all of physical creation for our survival. Your body does not end at the edges of your skin—it reaches beyond the physical boundaries into the air around you, which feeds your lungs; it stretches out through space to the Sun, which nourishes the soil with light and gives you food; it extends deep into the Earth, which offers you wood and rocks and earth to create shelter. In this way, your body goes on forever in all directions, and contains all things.

Your very existence is a product of an eternal cosmic courtship between Heaven and Earth. Can you not see how loved you are by your Father, the Sky, and your Mother, the Earth, who come together in every moment to bring you life? There is a meditation I teach my students in one of my seminars:

> "The Earth is my Mother,
> The Sky is my Father.
> I am a child of Universal Love . . ."

The next time you feel disconnected from the world around you, or you're looking for a real moment, go outside, sit down on some grass or dirt, and repeat this to yourself silently, or aloud, with your eyes open or closed. Between each repetition, take a deep breath, filling up with the gift of air. Soon, you will feel your connection to wholeness, and you will know peace.

✦

"People see God every day. They just don't recognize him."
— PEARL BAILEY

When we separate the spiritual from the everyday, we limit our opportunities for real moments. We miss ordinary miracles and wonders because we are looking for something flashy, something that screams "I am special, I am holy." We are so distracted by our search for the extraordinary that we don't even recognize the sacred when we encounter it.

The other day a good friend and I were talking about our own growth process, and he asked me if I believed that there were any truly holy people in the world. I thought for a minute, and answered that I believed *anytime a person was coming from a place of love and kindness, they were holy.* The Greek root of the word "holy" is *holos*, meaning complete or whole. **So holiness really is wholeness, and holy people are people in touch with their wholeness and the intrinsic wholeness of the Universe.**

I have learned that you don't have to look far for real moments of holiness. They are everywhere. All you need to do is to pay attention. . . .

One night a few months ago, my husband and I were coming out of a restaurant when we heard someone singing. We looked up and we saw a middle-aged man walking slowly along the sidewalk, carrying several shopping bags and crooning a lonesome song to himself. I thought perhaps he was just someone in a melancholy mood until he got closer—then I noticed that his clothes were threadbare, he appeared thin and hungry, and was shivering in the cold. "He probably doesn't have a home," I thought sadly. I realized that he had no intention of stopping and asking us for money. He was just passing by.

Something in this man's song touched my heart deeply, and I decided to reach out to him.

"You have a beautiful voice," I called out. He stopped and smiled at us.

"Thank you kindly," he answered. "It used to be better, but the damp air isn't too good for it."

"Would you sing some more for us?" we asked. And so he did, soft and shy at first, and then forgetting where and who he was, he sang boldly, belting out a hymn with all his heart and soul. For a moment, he was no longer a forgotten face on the boulevard, looking for a doorway to sleep in. He was an artist with an audience, sharing his gift with us, the only thing he had to share—the joy of song he had somehow managed to hold on to even though he had lost everything else. And as his voice soared, it filled the night with an ancient holiness, for in it, I heard the voices of every human being who had ever sung to God in delight, or darkness, or despair.

When he was done, we applauded and told him how good he truly was. Andy, for that was his name, apologized for only knowing a few verses of the song. "I haven't been too well lately," he explained. "I've had a lot of bad breaks, lost my job and my apartment, but I still try to keep a good attitude." As I listened to Andy talk about his unthinkably difficult life with a cheerful smile, I knew he had succeeded at something most people, including myself, find very difficult. In spite of every-thing, he still celebrated his joy in being alive. He was moving through life singing. He was having real moments.

Before Andy left, we gave him some money and wished him well. I know that we made a difference in his life, not so much because of the dollars we put in his hand, but because we allowed him, for a moment, to be somebody special and make a difference back to us. That night, we got the better half of the deal. *Andy was our teacher, our sidewalk angel, our unlikely but genuine holy man.* His unfailing spirit filled me with humility as I was reminded that with all the blessings in my life, I don't walk around singing joyfully as he does.

✦

Real moments of holiness happen when we experience moments of wholeness with ourself, our environment, or another person. **As you go through your day, look for holy moments and everyday miracles**—the hug your child gives you for no reason at all; a flock of birds flying past a cloud; the beautiful array of fruits and vegetables the earth has produced that are waiting for you at the supermarket; the song playing on the radio that gives you just the message you've been needing to hear; the lone yellow dandelion bursting through the crack in the concrete sidewalk.

When you stop and pay attention to holy
moments and everyday miracles, you will start
living with awe and wonder, and participating in
a Divine love affair with God.

Living Each Day with Reverence

My husband and I recently spent several weeks in Bali, an island which is part of Indonesia. The Balinese have a reputation for being the friendliest people on earth, and after getting to know some of them in our travels, I would say they are also the happiest. This is not because of what they have, because they have very little in terms of material possessions: The average income is around three hundred dollars per year; most Balinese live in open-air homes with no glass windows or solid doors; and the majority of them bathe and wash their clothing in the rivers and streams that surround the lush, green rice fields. But I would never call the people of Bali poor, *for they possess a rare gift of knowing how to truly enjoy and find sacred meaning in every moment of life, and this is the secret to their happiness. They are masters at creating real moments.*

Each morning Jeffrey and I would go to breakfast in the hotel restaurant, and there we would be greeted by Putu, our smiling waitress. Putu was one of the most content people I have ever met. Her eyes sparkled with joy, her manner radiated warmth and peace. When I first met her, we had just arrived from the United States, and in her presence I became even more aware of how tense, hurried, and agitated I was. I watched her move with grace, I listened to her laughter as she handed me a glass of juice, and I realized that Putu knew something that I did not. In spite of all my success, and the luxurious comforts we live with daily in the United States, I had to admit that Putu was a much happier person than I was. And she knew it too. "It is hard for us to understand," she shared with me in her careful English, "why all of the people who come here from America have so much, yet look so unhappy."

Putu told me this without judgment. She simply could not figure out what we tourists were doing in our everyday lives that had caused our hearts and spirits to be so much more closed than those of her friends and family who lived simply on the island. But after spending time on Bali, I knew the answer. I learned it from watching a tiny, withered couple in their eighties cheerfully working their rice paddy one day, as they had done for over sixty years, stopping to wave gaily at me as I walked by. I learned it from our guide Adi, who told me that every morning he woke up excited, waiting to discover what interesting people and beautiful sights God would put in his path as he drove us around. I learned it from a master wood craftsman in a tiny village, who treated each of his carved Buddhas like they were Lord Buddha himself, polishing their wood bellies with love.

All of these kind people have one thing in common—they live each day of their lives with joy and reverence. They thank the rice for growing as they harvest it; they thank the sun for rising as they walk out into its warmth; they take delight in each new person they meet; they celebrate each new day as a sacrament. *They are masters at everyday spirituality. The whole Earth is their temple, and their very existence reason enough to rejoice.*

My wonderful trip to Bali was a humbling and inspiring experience. Since I returned, I've been trying to live with more reverence for all life around me, and when I do, I find myself blessed with many more real moments.

✦

"A man asked his Rabbi, 'O wise one, how can I best serve God?' and waited for a profound reply. The old Rabbi thought for a moment and answered: 'You can best serve God with whatever you are doing in the moment.'"

—OLD HASIDIC STORY

Real moments with yourself do not occur when you do anything special or out of the ordinary, but, as the great sage Yogananda said, *when you do little things in an extraordinary way.* Do whatever you already do, but pay attention:

It is mindfulness that transforms the ordinary task into the extraordinary experience.

The "Right Now Meditation"

I want to share with you my favorite technique for living mindfully, but first, let me explain how it came about. One day about a year ago, I took my dog Bijou out for his afternoon stroll. I'd walked almost four blocks when I suddenly stopped and realized that I wasn't on the walk at all—I was thinking about a phone call I'd just finished with a TV producer; I was worrying about meeting my book deadline; I was wondering whether or not I should hire a new employee. I was everywhere but walking down the street. "Happiness can only be found in this moment," I reminded myself, "but how do I get myself back to this moment, and how do I stay once I get here?"

Suddenly, two words popped into my head: *"RIGHT NOW . . ."* I decided to use this phrase and fill in the sentence with whatever I was actually doing in the moment. This is how my thoughts went:

"Right now, I am walking Bijou up the hill. . . . Right now, I am placing one foot in front of the other onto the pavement. . . . Right now, I am watching Bijou's cute little body prance in front of me. . . . Right now, I am taking a deep breath of summer air. . . . Right now, I am looking up at the blue sky. . . . Right now I'm admiring that red flower. . . Right now, I am right here, right now. . . ."

As I practiced my *"Right Now Meditation,"* my mind relaxed, and my breathing deepened. I stopped trying to rush Bijou along, and enjoyed stopping whenever he did. I began to feel very centered in each moment, and a quiet sense of peace began to permeate my whole being. By the time our walk was over, I felt as if I'd just had a mini-vacation, and I wore a smile of contentment on my face.

Since that day, I practice *"Right Now Meditation"* all the time, especially when I am looking for a real moment.

Some Hints for Practicing "Right Now Meditation"

✦ Try doing it at least once a day.

✦ You can use this technique when you are driving, cooking, eating, people-watching, building something, taking a walk, making love, or doing anything at all.

✦ Do your series of "Right Now's" for at least five minutes to get the most benefits.

✦ Always end with the phrase:
   "RIGHT NOW, I AM RIGHT HERE, RIGHT NOW. . . ."

✦ It's good to take a deep relaxing breath between each "Right Now," because breathing always places you instantly in the moment.

✦ I've found the technique works best when you think your "Right Now's" silently to yourself, rather than saying them out loud. You may want to experiment.

Using "Right Now" as a Breathing Meditation

One variation of this mindfulness technique is to use it with your breathing when you are sitting quietly with your eyes closed. Find a comfortable place where you will not be disturbed. Close your eyes, and become aware of your breathing as you inhale, and as you exhale. Then begin your "Right Now Meditation" silently as follows:

AS YOU INHALE: "Right now, I am breathing in."
AS YOU EXHALE: "Right now, I am breathing out."
REPEAT . . .

You will notice that your breathing begins to slow down, become more even, and that the spaces between each inhalation and each exhalation are filled with a timeless peace. **Do not concentrate as you think your "Right Now's"** . . . just *gently* have the thought about breathing in and breathing out.

If you would like to use your "Right Now" breathing for some emotional healing, you can use these phrases:

AS YOU INHALE: "Right now, I am breathing in love."
AS YOU EXHALE: "Right now, I am breathing out fear."
REPEAT . . .

I've used this in seminars with wonderful results. You may even notice old buried emotions surfacing and clearing away, or long-unshed tears emerging from your eyes.

Other Techniques for Creating Real Moments with Yourself

✦ *Keep a Journal or Diary.* Don't write down events, but rather, record your uncensored feelings, your observations, your real moments. It's not necessary to write each day—even a few times a week will be valuable. *The more you put your attention on real moments you've just experienced, the more of them you will recognize the next time.*

✦ *Have an Inner Guidance Session with Yourself.* A variation on keeping a journal is to imagine that you are connected to a powerful source of wisdom and truth, whether you see it as a Guide or Teacher, or just an energy, and *ask it to send you messages you need to hear through the process of your writing.* Open yourself to whatever pops into your mind, and write down whatever you "hear" in your head. *Don't stop to analyze or understand what's coming out.* When you are finished, read what you've just "received"—you will be amazed at the quality of wisdom and inner guidance that poured through you onto the page.

✦ *Take a Mindfulness Walk.* Even if you don't have a dog, you need to take yourself for a walk once in a while. Instead of just going somewhere, make it a mindfulness walk by using the *"Right Now Meditation"* as you stroll along. You will notice things inside of you, and outside of you, that you hadn't been aware of before.

> "Just to be is a blessing.
> Just to live is holy."
> — RABBI ABRAHAM HESCHEL

Yesterday, approximately 200,000 people throughout the world died. Their time on Earth is over. They did not wake up this morning. They did not feel the sun on their face, or feel the wind on their skin. They did not hear laughter, or singing, or birds calling to each other. They could not eat an apple or drink a glass of water. They were not held or kissed or smiled at. They cannot see the stars twinkling in the sky tonight. They cannot gaze at the moon. They cannot read these words, close the book, turn out the light, and snuggle into the covers, only to dream and wake again.

You are alive.
You are here *now*.
You have another day.
That is a blessing.
Enjoy the ordinary everyday miracles that make
up your life. . . .
They will be your most sacred real moments.

· 12 ·

SILENCE AND SACRED SPACES

"We need to find God, and he cannot be found in noise and rest-lessness. God is the friend of silence."

— MOTHER TERESA

It is often in silence and solitude that you will find your most meaningful real moments. Silence nourishes the soul and heals the heart. It creates an insulated space between you and the noisy, demanding world you live in, a womb of still-ness in which you can be reborn over and over again. Silence has a regenerative power of its own. It is always sacred. It always returns you home.

Solitude is very necessary for silences which go deep. You must make time to be alone. Aloneness is not the same as loneliness. The word *alone* is derived from the Middle English phrase *"all one."* When you are alone, you are not simply away from others, but you are *with yourself,* **you are all one—** you are at one with your own essence; you come back to wholeness with yourself. In this way, you are not aware of the lack of the people from whom you've temporarily retreated— *you are aware of the fullness of you.* And it is in your *all oneness* that you can listen to your own inner voices, invite direction from your own guides, and recapture your own dreams.

The ancients knew the value of the solitary journey, the silent vigil by a fire, the vision quest. But we live in a time when technology has stolen our silence and solitude from us. It is increasingly difficult to find a truly quiet place. Even mountain stillness or desert tranquillity is regularly disturbed by the roar of jet planes overhead and the rumble of passing cars with radios blasting. It is hard to be completely alone with over five billion of us living on one planet.

Most of us have very little silence in our lives. Try recalling the last experience you had, excluding your sleep time, of being in silence for an hour or more. You wake up to your clock radio blaring, you watch television while you dress and eat, you drive to work listening to the morning talk show, you eat lunch in a noisy restaurant, and so the day goes. We get so used to the lack of silence that we become uncomfortable when faced with it. I have a friend who lives in New York City and travels quite frequently. He never leaves home without one item—his "noise machine," a device that emits a constant background noise that people play in order to sleep. Whenever he stays at my house, which is in the mountains outside of Los Angeles, he complains that "it's too quiet here—silence gives me the creeps." Then, he plugs in his little machine, and as he listens to the "noise," he falls easily asleep.

My friend's "creeps" come from the discomfort he experiences when the silence removes all of his distractions, draws his attention inward, and forces him to be with himself.

Silence and solitude are confrontational.
They plunge us instantly into truth,
and it is for this reason that they are so essential
to the health of our spirit.

Silence allows you to pay attention to everything, to watch the flow of mental garbage that goes through your mind. It's like sitting for a while on a riverbank and watching debris float by on the river. When you choose to be solitary and silent, you witness the thoughts, reactions, and emotions that have been interfering with your ability to make clear decisions, or to discover the answers to problems, or to know what your true feelings are. You can observe all of this emotional debris, notice what isn't serving you or is actually causing pain and turmoil in your life, and decide what you want to throw out and what you want to keep.

Imagine that you are hanging pictures in your living room. You become so absorbed in your task that you don't take time to stop, stand back, and notice if the pictures are hung correctly. You just keep banging those nails into the wall. Taking times for silence means standing back far enough so you can determine if the pictures in your life are crooked or straight. **Silence will help you see clearly, sometimes for the first time, exactly what is out of balance in your life.**

Going in makes coming out much
more powerful.

When you make the time for the apparent nondoing of silence and solitude, your doing will become much more effective and meaningful. Great sages, shamans, saints, and warriors have always known this. They retreated into silence before undertaking a journey, a battle, a ceremony, a quest. They took their solitude on hilltops under the full moon, in hidden groves deep in the forest, in sweat lodges, in chapels. There, they would empty themselves of their limitations and burdens, and open to the sacred mystery of the void. They would be transported beyond the constraints of time and space. They would be embraced by the life-giving power that is the Source of all creation. And then, they would emerge to perform their earthly responsibilities, infused with power and vision that can only be acquired from contact with the Unbounded.

In my own life, it is the silences that have formed the foundation for the creations and contributions I am most proud of. When I was in my twenties, I spent months at a time on meditation courses in Europe with other meditation teachers. We would often practice days, and even weeks of silence along with our regular meditations. For weeks at a time, I wouldn't utter a sound, nor would I hear one—no conversations, no greetings, no jokes . . . just silence. The deeper I went into silence, the more profound my spiritual experiences became.

Looking back, I know that these were some of the most powerful and transformational moments of my life, preparing me for the work I was to do in the years to come. My husband teases me and says, "Yes, but once you came out of silence, you started talking, and haven't stopped since!!" In some ways he is correct. I went so deep within myself, like pulling an arrow back on the bow, that I often feel I am still flying through the air in the other direction. I do know that without those opportunities to travel deeply inward, I would never have been able to come out into the world with such determination and focus, and I wouldn't have known how to listen to the forces that have guided me.

✦

"The more you talk about It,
the more you think about It,
the further from It you go.
Stop talking, stop thinking,
and there is nothing you will not understand . . ."
— SENGSTAN

The power of silence lies in its emptiness. *Silence is a receptive space. It creates a sacred void, an opening through which you can receive: truth, perspective, strength, healing, revelation.* In silence, you transcend words, and contact the wordless. You transcend form, and contact the formless. You fill up with a peaceful knowing.

Silence is not the same as prayer. Prayer is a way of directing your feelings and thoughts, focusing them and sending them toward a source. Silence is listening, receiving, being. One is trying to reach the source or communicate with it; the other, silence, is allowing yourself to hear the source within yourself, to become one with it. Prayer is directed outward. Silence is directed inward. **In prayer, you are the sender; but in silence, you are the receiver.**

I believe that God, Goddess, Cosmic Intelligence, The Higher Power, or whatever force you believe in is there to be called upon, thanked, and appreciated. **But I also believe that communication with Spirit is like a two-way radio, that you can receive messages as well as you can send them out.** *If you aren't feeling as connected as you'd like to Spirit, and you've been praying in the traditional way as hard as you can, perhaps you need to pray less and listen more. Maybe God's been waiting for a chance to talk to you, but hasn't been able to get in a word edgewise . . . !*

Learning to Listen to Silence

Navigating through silence is like navigating the ocean—it is a skill. It takes practice, and the more you practice, the better you get. *The first step is to quiet your mind, to leave behind your usual thought processes.* That's like getting into a boat that takes you away from the shore and out to sea. Just as there are many kinds of boats, there are many methods for quieting the mind. You can use any one of a variety of meditation techniques and breathing exercises. Take the time to find one that works for you. After all, if you don't like your boat, you won't want to go out sailing very often.

Once you have your vehicle for traveling away from your everyday landscape, you will need to learn to become a master at grabbing on to the currents and riding the waves. There are different "waves" or levels of silence:

. . . There is surface silence, a quiet, gentle calm that lulls you into a centered space.

. . . There is deep silence, a powerful swirling rush of love and knowingness that sends your spirit rocking and rolling into new levels of consciousness.

. . . And then, there is the tidal wave of silence, an overwhelming force that engulfs you completely, swallowing up your ego and identity, and plunging you into a swirling mass of Light and Bliss, until you become one with it.

Start wherever you are, and let the Silence itself become your guide. It will take you wherever you need to go.

✦

If you aren't used to going within, you will need to be patient with yourself while you learn how to navigate inner space. It will take you some time to get used to its rhythms and melodies:

Imagine you are walking through the woods with a friend who happens to be carrying a portable tape player that's blasting loud music. You won't be able to hear anything else but the music. If your friend turns the tape off, at first you still won't hear much—your ears need to adjust to the quiet. Soon, you will start to notice sounds that were always there, the rustle of leaves in the wind, tiny animals moving through the brush, the creak of massive tree branches. The more time you spend listening, the more you will hear.

It is the same with taking journeys inside yourself. At first, it may seem like nothing is happening, like you are just sitting there breathing or meditating. Soon, however, you will learn to pick up feelings that are very quiet, but were always there beneath the everyday noisiness of the mind.

> When you and the silence become friends, it
> will speak to you as loudly as anything you could
> ever hear from the outer world. Soon, you will
> not be able to ignore its voice, which, after all,
> is the voice of your own spirit calling to you.

Here are a few other very simple ways to experience more silence in your life:

✦ **Drive with your radio turned off.** *Cars are great moving meditation centers.* You can't be bothered, and you can't really get up and leave. Some of my greatest revelations have come while driving in my car. For twelve years I gave a weekend seminar once a month in Los Angeles, and each Friday night on the way to the workshop, I would drive in total silence, allowing my mind to empty and to tune in to my inner broadcast. I've also taken many wonderful long car trips in silence, especially when I'm traveling out of town. By the time I arrived at my destination, I had received guidance I needed and answers I'd been searching for.

Make your car into a sacred space: When you are alone, try driving silently, or listening to gentle music that has no lyrics. Keep your eyes on the road, but listen for the sound of your inner voice.

✦ **Sit in silence by firelight or candlelight.** Build a fire in your fireplace, or simply light some candles, place them close to you on a table or desk where you can see them, and turn out the lights. Make sure the TV and radio are turned off, and that you won't be disturbed. Sit and watch the flames. Listen to the logs crackle, or watch the wax drip down the side of the candle. Imagine the light illuminating all of the dark or hidden places inside of you. Pay attention to what you see. Or if you see nothing, just enjoy the simplicity of the moment.

✦ **Take a silent walk with the person you love.** This is a way of sharing your silence. Find an enjoyable place to walk, the quieter the better. Hold hands. Feel the rhythm of each other's footsteps, the warmth of their skin touching yours. Pay attention to everything you see, and everything you feel. Soon, you may notice that your hearts are speaking a silent language with one another.

✦

"Your sacred space is where you can find yourself again and again."
—JOSEPH CAMPBELL

I believe that each of us needs a sacred space, a symbolic environment which draws our awareness in and focuses it on our true journey. Having your own sacred space will help you experience more real moments in your life. It will call you back to the real moments you have had before, and make your pilgrimage within easier.

A sacred space can be a pillow in the corner of your bedroom where you pray or meditate, a shelf or dresser where you place objects that have special meaning, even a wall where you hang reminders of your growth process. It should be someplace you can sit or kneel in front of, or if that's not possible, a place you can stand in front of. It doesn't have to be big—it might only be a six-inch by six-inch section of your night table.

A space is made sacred by your intention that it be so.

That is it. You do not need fancy statues or the perfect piece of furniture. All you need is whatever you would like to have there, things that will help center you and stir your spirit. Your sacred space might include:

✦ Photographs of people you love—your mate, children, friends, family, pets
✦ Photographs of beloved relatives who have passed on
✦ Religious or spiritual symbols that have meaning for you
✦ Pictures of your guides and teachers
✦ Mementos from your life that remind you of special real moments
✦ Your favorite inspirational books, your Bible, prayer book, etc.
✦ Objects from nature that will remind you of your connection to the Earth: rocks, crystals, flowers, shells, etc.
✦ Candles

My sacred space is in my writing room at home. I am looking at it right now. It is on the top of a low cabinet against the window. It contains many of the items I listed, and others that are precious to me. It is the place where I pray, where I center myself, where I ask for guidance, where I express gratitude for my blessings. I have my own special, private rituals I perform there, rituals that are designed to help me turn within and remember who I really am and what I am here for. Whenever I feel lost or frightened, whenever I move off center, I come upstairs to my sacred space, kneel or sit before it, and use it to guide me back home to myself.

Even when I'm traveling, I create a little sacred space wherever I am. The first thing I do when I arrive in a hotel room is to take out a few special objects and place them next to my bed. Now the room is mine, now I am at peace.

Some people like to have another sacred space outdoors. If

you are fortunate enough to live in an environment where this is possible, your outdoor sacred space might be a special tree behind your house, or a spot by a lake, or a rock over-looking the ocean. You can bring important objects with you on your visits, or you can come alone and simply allow the sanctity of Mother Nature herself to help you return to center.

Don't be in a hurry to create a sacred space where you live if you don't already have one. Just hold the intention of invit-ing it into your life, and then wait for a while. *Let your sacred space tell you where it wants to be.* Slowly, it will manifest itself as one object after another finds its way there. Some will be things you've had for a long while. Some will be unexpected gifts. In time, you will construct your own unique rituals and real moments in your sacred space.

The more you visit your physical sacred space,
the more you will get into the habit of
connecting with your inner sacred space, until
soon, you will carry your sacred space with you
wherever you go.

✦

"Come out of the circle of time
And into the circle of love."
—JALALUDIN RUMI

The easiest way to make any space a place where you can experience real moments is to bring love to it. **Love makes every space sacred, and every moment meaningful.** When you and your partner lie in bed at night and hold each other close, you are in a sacred space. When you are brushing out your daughter's hair, you are in a sacred space. When you offer a hug to a friend who is filled with sadness, you are in a sacred space. Love ushers us into a timeless place of rapture. While we are immersed in loving, love is all there is. Nothing else exists.

After you read this, close your eyes.
Breathe gently and deeply, until you have pulled
your awareness from the outside in.
Navigate past your thoughts, and around
your feelings.
Keep going, until you find the Silence.
Dive in . . . go deeper and deeper.
Now, float in the Silence.
Let it permeate every cell of your being.
Know it as Peace.
Know it as Love.
Become the silence. . . .

· 13 ·

RITUALS AND
REAL MOMENTS

"When humans participate in ceremony, they enter a sacred space. Everything outside of that space shrivels in importance. Time takes on a different dimension. Emotions flow more freely. The bodies of participants become filled with the energy of life, and this energy reaches out and blesses the creation around them. All is made new; everything becomes sacred."

— SUN BEAR

Rituals create powerful opportunities for you to experience real moments. They transport you from the regular everyday world into the world of the sacred, and help reconnect you with the wholeness of life. When you practice a ritual or personal ceremony, you instantly become conscious and mindful. You create a sacred time and space, as each act is rich with significance. You are right here, right now, remembering your true purpose, nourishing your heart, and renewing your spirit.

For as long as human beings have walked the earth, we have made ritual a part of our lives. Those ancient ones who came before us and lived in harmony with the earth understood the importance of the sacred ceremony as a path for creating connection, and for infusing what was often a harsh and challenging existence with higher meaning. There were rituals for planting the crop, and rituals for celebrating the harvest. There were rituals to honor the change of seasons, and rituals to honor the changes in our bodies. Dancing, singing, chanting, feasting, purifying, and praying were not practiced at random—they happened at prescribed times for a particular purpose.

Slowly, as the centuries progressed, we disconnected from the earth and shifted from living a spiritual existence to a more secular existence. And in the process, we removed much of the ritual from our lives. We were too busy trying to achieve more and become more to stop and perform ceremonies that did not create the instant results to which we had become addicted.

Some rituals were left, but especially here in America, they too were tainted by our materialistic values. Birthdays, Christmas, and anniversaries became about receiving gifts and eating and drinking too much, not about celebrating love and renewal. Weddings became about having a lavish party, not about consecrating the union of two hearts. Even death doesn't escape this siege by commercialism as we spend large sums of money on elaborate coffins and headstones, but don't take the time to fully honor and bless the spirit of our friend or relative.

When our life is devoid of ritual, we rush through it. *We don't stop to reflect on the meaning of the events that are happening to us. We find it hard to remember our purpose in the bigger scheme of things. We forget who we are. We lose our way.*

When our rituals turn away from the spiritual
and emotional and focus only on the material,
our spirits lose the roads on which they can
travel homeward.

✦

I had to travel thousands of miles across the world to witness an example of the life-enhancing power of ritual, on our recent trip to Bali. The Balinese have rituals and ceremonies for everything—there are rituals for opening your place of business each morning, rituals for blessing the bridges so that vehicles will travel safely across, rituals for the moment when your child takes his first steps. As our gentle and kindhearted guide, Adi, drove my husband and me through the lush rice fields and hills of the island, he explained all of the special prayers and ceremonies to us with reverence. *"Rituals give us the opportunity to focus our attention on what is important,"* he said humbly.

The spiritual peace one feels on Bali comes from the strong sense of meaning with which the Balinese do everything in their lives. Unlike many of us in the Western world, they do not wait for a few days a year on which they celebrate their children, or the food the earth provides, or the love of their family—they honor the blessings in their simple, harmonious existence daily. **Each day becomes a series of very real and significant moments.**

✦

What are rituals for?

✦ Rituals give rhythm to life.

They are the drumbeat keeping time as you walk on your path. They provide continuity. They offer predictable intervals in an unpredictable world. In this way, your acts of observance serve as a single thread that weaves itself through your days and nights, connecting you with the familiar. The prayer you say each morning as you greet the dawn, the ceremony of recommitment you and your beloved have on each anniversary, the solitary walk you take each Sunday—these become the milestones by which you measure your journey. *They stop and demand that you pay attention to the place where you are, the emotions you are feeling, and the moment you are in.*

On the last day of every year, Jeffrey and I celebrate a special ritual. We spend several hours sitting together in a quiet place and expressing our gratitude for everything that has happened to us in the past twelve months. We acknowledge each other as well as the other people who have given us love; we share our appreciation for the events that have occurred, the lessons we've learned, the challenges we've faced and the new wisdom they brought. Month by month, we go through the year and recall significant moments, lovely memories, and wonderful blessings. By the time New Year's Eve arrives, we feel fortunate and full of grace.

It is sad that so many people choose to pass through life's significant moments by getting so intoxicated that all they are left with the next day is a hangover. This, too, is a sort of ceremony, but *one that is based on becoming unconscious, not more conscious.* Our New Year's Eve ritual leaves us feeling complete with the year that has passed, and excited about the new year to come. We end the year with some very real moments, which is the best natural high of all.

✦ *Rituals are for celebrating rebirth, for marking passage from one stage of life to another.*

They are important for honoring the crossing of a symbolic threshold. We use them to acknowledge the obvious life changes—birth, marriage, and death—but there are so many other significant occasions that go unnoticed, and therefore, unsanctified: *the formation of a step-family; the changing of a career; moving from one home to another; the triumph over an* addiction; the healing of a disease or accident; the onset of menstruation, and, later, menopause; divorce or the letting go of a relationship; the last child leaving home; the accomplishment of a long-sought-after goal. By marking these experiences with ritual, they become intensely meaningful real moments.

A few years ago, when Jeffrey and I began talking about getting married, I found myself feeling very anxious and afraid. I knew the reason why—I still carried so much pain from my failed relationships that I felt "ruined," like damaged goods. I wished I'd never been married before, that I could come to him as if it were the first time. Turning the clock back was impossible, so I decided to create a passage ritual for myself, to officially end the cycle of pain I'd been in for so many years, and mark the new cycle of fulfillment.

I went to a special spot on a hill overlooking the ocean, where I could sit by myself. With me, I brought pictures of each man I'd loved, and some mementos from those relationships. I also brought some special objects from my sacred space at home that always help me connect with the higher truth. And then, I had my own "letting go" ritual, where I thanked each of those men for the lessons they taught me and the love they gave, took back whatever pieces of myself I felt I'd given each of them, and said good-bye to the past. I tore up the pictures and letters, and burned them in a little bowl until they were just ashes. Taking the ashes in my hands, I offered them back to the earth and the wind, and asked that my heart be healed of any fear of commitment, and be made whole again so I could offer all of it to Jeffrey.

This ritual marked my passage from the woman I had been to the woman I had become. *It gave me a moment to fully acknowledge my transformation, and to formally release the past.* Afterward, I felt like I'd shed one thousand pounds of fear. Of course, I continued to work on building up my trust in myself and strengthening our relationship, but that ceremony was a turning point in my healing process.

Perhaps you've passed through many life stages without stopping to honor your journey, or perhaps you are passing through an important stage right now. Take the time to create a meaningful ritual for yourself, and to celebrate your rebirth.

✦ *Rituals are for healing and renewal.*

They can be used to purify and strengthen your connection to God, your partner, your work, and yourself. You can create a renewal ritual when you feel the need for new clarity and strength, when you need guidance and direction, or when you and someone you love want to go to a deeper level of intimacy together, but feel there are some things in the way.

I do renewal rituals before I write a book, when I notice myself feeling spiritually disconnected and too caught up in my work, and when I come up against some old emotional pain that I am moving through too slowly. Sometimes I create them in my sacred space at home; sometimes I do them in the bathtub if I want to feel really "cleansed"; sometimes I go out in Nature to a mountaintop, or, when I can, to one of my favorite power spots like the one in Sedona, Arizona, that's pictured on this book cover. I always emerge from my renewal rituals feeling centered and protected.

✦

> "Only within burns the fire I kindle.
> My heart the altar.
> My heart the altar."
> — POEM OF A BUDDHIST NUN

All rituals begin and end in the heart. They are not about places; they are not about objects. They are about love, respect, and remembering.

Anything done with mindfulness and intention is a form of

ritual. In creating your own rituals, don't get caught up in the material trappings and forget your purpose—to create a moment of spiritual connection and meaningful awareness. You don't need to be surrounded by candles and incense, or be in any particular locale, or use some special formula if you choose not to. All you need is your decision to make the time and place you're in significant, and the experience you are having sacred.

> What makes a moment into a ritual? It is your intention that your time be ritualized and purposeful. It is your decision to give meaning to what you are doing.

Each of us needs to rediscover and redefine our own rituals. Some you will practice daily, some at special times. Here are a few *concepts* that will bring meaning to some of our traditional occasions for celebration. What kind of rituals you use and how you structure them is up to you.

Birthdays—Celebrate the birth of the person you've become in the past year. Give gratitude for another year of life, and for all the blessings you received. Release everything you don't want to take into the new year ahead. Honor your parents for coming together and giving you a passage onto the Earth.

Relationship Anniversaries—Celebrate the growth you've made as a couple in the past year. Honor each other for the love and devotion you've given. Acknowledge the changes you've seen in your partner. Recommit to your relationship, renew old vows, and create new ones for the coming year.

Baby Shower—Each person can share their wishes and wisdom for both mother and child, giving gifts of knowledge, as opposed to mere physical offerings. Tell the unborn baby how much it is loved and its birth anxiously awaited.

Thanksgiving—Share your gratitude for the blessings of the year. Make gratitude calls and write gratitude letters. Thank the Earth for providing you with a home and for sustaining you with its food.

Christmas/Hanukkah/New Year's Time—Celebrate the blessings of the year, the love you have received, and the light that has guided your life. Share your gratitude and love with those you care about. Give. Usher in the new cycle with joy.

Easter/Passover—Release anything you want to let go of, those parts of you that you no longer need or that don't serve your highest good. Say good-bye to the part of your old self that is dying, and welcome the resurrection of your new self as it begins its journey toward more freedom.

Vacations—Set goals for personal and spiritual renewal. Have the intention of not returning with certain burdens, tensions, or emotional blocks you left with. Use your time away for healing and reconnection with yourself and your loved ones.

✦

Our planet, our home, knows the secret of ritual and celebration. Each morning, the sun rises in a blaze of reds and oranges to kiss the Earth with light and warmth; birds sing their first jubilant song thanking the day, and gardens open in a colorful greeting. Each evening, the sun sets, painting the sky with a dramatic good-bye, and making way for the darkness; crickets chirp their rhythmic lullaby, and the Earth sleeps. Each winter, the Earth humbly sheds the old so the new can grow. Each spring, it proudly celebrates its renewal with an abundance of life.

The Earth does not allow its changes to go unheralded. It honors them with glorious and dramatic ritual. We must learn from the Earth, and honor our own cycles with sacred celebration. *It is showing us the way.*

If you live life in a sacred and mindful way,
every moment can be a ceremony
that honors your connection with the Creator
and with all living things. . . .

·14·

GRATITUDE AND
ACTS OF KINDNESS

"We can do no great things—only small things with great love."
— MOTHER TERESA

Several years ago, a woman named Anna Herbert from Marin County, California, became aware of a phrase running through her mind:

"Practice random kindness and senseless acts of beauty."

She began sharing this thought with friends, calling it a form of "positive anarchy," and decided to experiment with its philosophy by doing kind deeds at random. She would plant flowers in an ugly vacant lot; she'd pay the toll on the bridge for several cars behind her. Soon, the idea spread onto automobile bumper stickers, and across the country, and the "guerrilla kindness" movement was born.

Acts of kindness create instant real moments. They are the living rituals of everyday spirituality. They connect your heart with the heart of another person, and create pathways through which your love can flow.

The wonderful thing about practicing random kindness is that each day, you will be presented with thousands of opportunities to do so. A car will be waiting to be let into your lane of the highway; a person will be running to catch the elevator you're standing in; someone will drop some things and need help picking them up. You have children who need to be told they are special, a mate who needs to be told he/she is loved, friends who could use a one-minute phone call just to say you treasure them, dogs and cats who crave a hug, scratch, and a kiss, and hundreds of strangers to whom a smile would mean they were not invisible.

✦

Two years ago, Jeffrey and I rented a little cottage on a small island for our annual end-of-the-year vacation. The first day after we arrived, I had just sat down outside to read when I heard the pitiful "meow" of a cat who sounded like it was crying. When I looked in the bushes, I saw her—a scrawny stray black kitty that was more skin and bones than fur. She looked like she hadn't eaten in weeks, and was shaking from fear and hunger. I knew if I fed her, she wouldn't leave us alone for the next ten days, but my heart broke as I thought of her starving. I went inside, got a can of tuna fish, and placed it where she could see it.

For twenty minutes, the cat cried and whined, but wouldn't come near the food. She was terrified, I realized—she had gotten used to being yelled at and chased away by all of the local tourists, and didn't trust that I wouldn't hurt her as well. I sat on the ground and talked to her in a soothing voice, promising that I would take care of her if she would give me a chance.

Finally, my kitty friend cautiously approached the tuna, wolfed it down as fast as she could, and ran off into the bushes. But I knew she'd be back, and she was . . . later that day, just in time for dinner. I was prepared. I'd gone to the local store and stocked up on cat food, and it only took her five minutes to feel safe enough to eat it.

For the next week and a half, I took care of my small black friend. She spent much of her day lounging in the sun with us, and a few times at night when it rained, I'd hear her calling to me, and I'd unlock the door to our porch so she could have a dry place to sit out the storm. I looked forward to getting up each morning and seeing her little face peeking out from behind a bush. Jeffrey kept reminding me that when we left, the next tenant would probably chase her away again, but I didn't want to think about it.

The fateful day finally arrived when we were scheduled to leave and return home. Kitty watched us pack, walking in and out of my legs as if to say "Please don't go." I wrote a note for whoever was coming to the cottage next, begging them to feed the cat, and leaving them extra cans of food. But as we stood by the front gate with our suitcases, and Kitty planted herself in front of me, her green eyes staring into mine, I began to cry. "I'm abandoning her," I thought bitterly to myself. "I know I can't bring her back to the United States, but now that I've given her love, I'm being cruel by taking it away. Maybe she would have been better off if I hadn't given her a taste of kindness at all."

Suddenly, I heard a voice in my head whisper: *"You showed her what kindness was for the first time in her life. She will always take that with her. She will always know that she was loved. Love is never wasted."*

I'll never know what happened to my little black kitty friend. I hope she was cared for by someone else. But I do know this—with her help, I experienced many real and precious moments during that vacation. My love and kindness, however briefly they were shared, did make a difference in her life. And her love made a difference in mine.

Love and kindness are never wasted.
They always make a difference.
They bless the one who receives them,
and they bless you, the giver.

There are innumerable ways to create real moments by sharing your kindness: You can make sandwiches, drive by a city park, and give them out to the homeless people who live there; you can leave a daisy on a stranger's windshield; you can tell the person who is waiting on you in a restaurant that they are doing a great job. You don't even have to do anything physical—just sending people your kind thoughts and surrounding them with love will also affect them positively. When you see someone who appears to be unhappy or alone, visualize them surrounded by light and love. When you think of someone who is suffering or lost, wrap them in loving energy.

Never underestimate the healing power of everyday kindness. One loving word can lift a person out of the depths of despair and offer them hope; one smile can help them believe that they matter; one caring action can even save their life. I've personally met dozens of people who've confided to me that they were seriously contemplating suicide until a stranger said hello to them in an elevator, or a friend called to say "I was thinking about you." One real moment of love was enough to make the difference.

If each of you reading this practiced just one random act of kindness a day, starting tomorrow, our world would be transformed.

✦

"We are all connected to everyone and everything in the universe. Therefore, everything one does as an individual affects the whole. All thoughts, words, images, prayers, blessings, and deeds are listened to by all that is."

—SERGE KAHILI KING

Yesterday, I climbed a mountain. When I reached the top, I sat on a flat place between two tall stone spires, and looked out across the horizon. The day was clear, and I could see for miles: ancient red rock canyons, monuments to the massive earth changes that formed this beautiful part of the Southwestern United States; rolling hills alive with cactus, desert brush, and wildflowers; and sky—turquoise blue that seemed to stretch forever. The wind blew in strong gusts, kissing the mountain and me with its warm, sweet breath. Two hawks hovered almost motionless in the air above my head, their wings spread wide to catch the breeze, as if they, too, were awestruck by the glory of this place and this perfect afternoon.

I had come to the mountain looking for a real moment, and I had found one. Everything else but where I was and what I was experiencing dissolved, and I was left only with gratitude as I beheld the marvelous grace of the Creator. I was grateful that a spot such as this existed. I was grateful that my legs were strong enough to climb the steep hills to bring me here. I was grateful that I had eyes clear enough to see such an exquisite display of divine handiwork. I was grateful for my beloved husband and spiritual traveling companion, whose presence I could feel on a nearby ledge. I was grateful that I had been guided and protected thus far in my life so that I could arrive at this very moment.

My heart filled with quiet joy. My mind emptied and opened to peace. And one phrase echoed through my body: *"Thank you. . . ."*

> Ultimately, real moments are always
> moments of gratitude.

You cannot have a real moment without feeling truly grateful. Just the fact that you here, that you are able to experience a real moment doing whatever you are doing, will fill you with gratitude. *Your very existence is a miracle, as is the world you live in.* You do not have to be on a mountaintop to feel grateful. Anytime you stop for a moment, and pay complete and mindful attention to the fact of your presence here on Earth, your spirit will whisper "Thank you."

✦

If you want to experience a real moment, and remember nothing else you've read in these pages, simply begin focusing on your gratitude. Find something you feel grateful for, and then let yourself really feel it. Maybe you're grateful that your children are healthy and safe. Maybe you're grateful for the love a friend continually shows you. Maybe you're grateful that you woke up in a comfortable bed and had something to eat. Maybe you're grateful that you've survived this long in spite of your own efforts to self-destruct. Surrender completely to the feeling of gratitude, and you will be having a real moment.

> When you live with constant gratitude,
> your life will become a living prayer.

We often think of prayer as an asking, a plea to a higher power for a favor or blessing. And there is a time and a place when we need to request guidance and strength. But the word *pray* really means *"to praise."* From the beginning of time, man and woman have known the power of prayer as a means to give thanks for the wonder of creation, to honor the gift of life. This kind of prayer, then, becomes a vehicle through which our gratitude can flow forth. It connects us with our love for living, and reminds us of the abundance of real moments that are continually bestowed upon us.

Sun Bear, a sacred Native American teacher and author, says that prayer is a way "for humans to give back to the creation some of the energy they are always receiving." The Earth gives us a home on which to place our feet; the air allows us to breathe; the water sustains us; the Sun keeps us warm and illuminates our path with light. Gratitude allows us to put life back in balance.

How can our prayers and praises affect the Universe? They are an energy, a vibration of love, and all vibration affects everything else in creation. *When you feel gratitude in your heart, you are loving creation in a very concrete way.*

The Earth is a living, breathing organism. Like you, like anything that is alive, it too needs to be treated with love and kindness. How easily we forget that we are guests on this planet, that Mother Earth generously gives of herself for our comfort and pleasure. *If a friend invited you to be a guest in her home, would you throw your trash on her floor? Would you put poison in her water supply? Would you tear down her walls so you could make room for your own possessions? Would you kill her pets so you could have more space to yourself, or because you thought it was fun?*

This is how we have been treating our planet, like rude, insensitive house guests who mistakenly think we can leave whenever we want to. But this is our home. There is nowhere else for us to go.

We must stop taking our loving host, Mother Earth, for granted. We must behave like any decent guest would—*we should respect the space we have been given; we should clean up after ourselves; we should offer our help where it is needed; and most of all, we should learn to say "Thank you."*

✦

Begin by saying "Thank you" to creation whenever you can. You can start right now. . . .

    . . . If you have a window nearby, look outside, notice the trees, or the other people who keep you company here on the

Earth, or the daylight that allows you to see all of this beauty, and say "*Thank you.*" Say it out loud. It will feel good. It will make you smile.

. . . If you are at home, and have a refrigerator full of food that the Earth has generously provided, open the door, look at the amazing variety of delicious nourishment, and say "*Thank you.*"

. . . Walk into your children's bedroom. Watch them sleeping. Somehow they were created out of your body, through the brilliant design of divine intelligence. Kiss their foreheads, pull up their covers, and say "*Thank you.*"

. . . Take a deep breath. Feel the air slide into your lungs, feeding your body with life. Exhale, and everything you don't need is released. Breathe in again—there's enough air for every breath you need to take, and it's the perfect formula to keep you alive. Exhale again, and say "*Thank you.*"

Thank you for reading my words, and receiving the love behind them. Thank you for traveling with me, and coming this far on our journey. We are almost home. . . .

· 15 ·

FINDING YOUR WAY
BACK HOME

"I searched for God and all I found was myself.
I searched for myself and all I found was God."
— SUFI QUOTE

What is your true destination on your journey Home? It is nowhere but here, no time but now. It is in this moment alone that you can find yourself. It is in this moment alone that you can find God. *That is because there is always nothing else but this moment, and this moment, and this moment.*

I have spent my whole life learning how to get back to this moment, to where I already am. Slowly, slowly, more and more of me is arriving here as I reclaim the pieces of my spirit that ran away from home. One by one, they return from their quest for what they thought would make me happy, only to find that happiness cannot be acquired—it can only be learned.

When I look for happiness, I lose it. When I
stop looking, and surrender to where I am,
I find it.

Like this, we are all forgetting who we are, and remembering, and forgetting over and over again. That is the journey, not a straight line from here to there, but a circle, from here to here, and back around. But each time, the forgetting becomes less painful, and the remembering easier.

Someone once explained to me that our spiritual growth unfolds in the same way an eagle rises from the ground toward the sky. He does not fly straight upward. He circles, passing over the same territory again and again, but each time, from a higher vantage point. This is how we come home—we slowly rise into the fullness and freedom of who we truly are, until finally, we become one with the Truth.

The Talmud says *"Every blade of grass has its angel that bends over it and whispers, 'Grow, grow . . .'"* You, too, are being guided and protected on your journey home. Teachers will appear when you need them, and when you are ready. They already have. Some you will recognize, others you may not. Don't forget that teachers come in all forms, and some of the best ones may not look like teachers at all.

The task of your teachers is not to take you anywhere, but to help you pay attention to where you are. Know that the more you surrender into each moment, the sooner you will be able to experience all of the love and peace that is waiting for you right here.

✦

"What would it be like if you lived each day, each breath, as a work of art in progress? Imagine that you are a Masterpiece unfolding, every second of every day, a work of art taking form with every breath."

—THOMAS CRUM

It is evening, at dusk. I find myself drawn to the backyard of my home from where I can watch the fog float in from the sea, following the valley that lies between my hill and the wilderness across from me. The sky is violet and flame. The only sounds are the night birds chanting in rhythm like contented monks. Everywhere there is stillness.

I sit with my dog in my lap and marvel at nature's exquisite way of saying good night. And then, I think to myself: *"It will always be like this here, even in forty or fifty years when I am no longer alive to witness it. The same fog will appear at sunset on hot summer days, and fill the night with mist. The same sea will lie quietly in the distance. The same trees will send shadows across the lawn. The same moon will rise through above the clouds, painting the valley silver with its light. All of this will be here, but I will be gone."*

For several minutes, I am overwhelmed by the eternality of nature. I feel small, frightened, and hopeless in my insignificance. What can possibly have meaning in my life? What can I possibly do or accomplish that will make sense?

My dog shifts on my lap to get a better view. Suddenly, I remember that all I am supposed to do is what I'm doing:

To stop, sit back, and witness the glorious spectacle of creation. . . .

To receive the privilege and blessing of being alive. . . .

To be fully present, right here, right now. . . .

To love. . . . To be grateful. . . .

To celebrate life, moment by moment. . . .

I am part of the sacred ritual taking place. . . .
I am part of what makes it beautiful. . . .

May your life be rich with real moments
and
may you travel your path in peace. . . .